How Domestic Animals Came to the United States

By Lyle Gingerich

DEDICATION

To Ferdinand the Bull, who had the sense to stay in Spain.

ACKNOWLEDGEMENTS

I would like to thank the Iowa State University Parks Library, Veterinary Medical Library, Special Collections Department, Periodical Reference Section and Inter-library Loan Services for assistance in compiling the references for this work.

CHAPTERS

PREFACE

There were almost no domestic animals in the United States until they were brought by European explorers and settlers. The ancestors of every cow, horse, sheep, dog, house cat, chicken and goat came to the United States on a boat. Many of the original imports came from Spain in the 1500's. Later, domestic animals came from other European countries.

Domestic animals are so common in the United States that the thought of the country without them seems unreal. Yet, it is a fact. There were semi-domesticated dogs, but no truly domestic animals. Mexico had domestic turkeys**. Canada had semi-domesticated reindeer.

The native animals in the United States weren't acceptable for domestication. Bears have never been tamed; cougars likewise. Buffalo, despite numerous efforts, have not succeeded as farm animals. Even the buffalo/cow combination – a biological match – has resulted in a nasty-tempered beast that is unruly to handle on a farm. Mountain goats can't be raised successfully. Foxes, coyotes, deer, elk and antelope have not been domesticated.

This book tells where and when domestic animals, including dogs, were introduced to the United States, how they escaped, how they behaved in the wild and where significant populations of these animals ran free.

Domestic animals are more wild than tame. They prefer to live in the wild despite being domesticated for more than 10,000 years, in some cases. (See Table Below)

This book is organized by type of animal. Each chapter can be read independently. It starts with cattle, the species with the widest range and the most individual animals running wild at one time.

** Relatively new archeological evidence shows that there may have been domesticated turkeys in the U.S. Southwest. (1)

DATES OF ANIMAL DOMESTICATION (ZEDER)

COW
DOMESTICATED 7000 B.C.
TO U.S. IN 1540 and 1565
WENT WILD IN FLORIDA, TEXAS, EAST COAST, SOUTH, CALIFORNIA, GREAT PLAINS, HAWAII AND ALASKA

HORSE
DOMESTICATED 3600 B.C.
TO U.S. IN 1521
WENT WILD IN FLORIDA, TEXAS, EAST COAST, GREAT PLAINS, CALIFORNIA

PIG
DOMESTICATED 7000 B.C.
TO U.S. IN 1539
WENT WILD IN ALL STATES

DONKEY
DOMESTICATED 4000 B.C.
TO U.S. IN 1565
WENT WILD IN SOUTHWEST AND WEST

CHICKEN
DOMESTICATED 6000 B.C.
TO KAUAI 700 A.D., TO U.S. 1500s
WENT WILD: URBAN ESCAPES AND HAWAII

CAMEL
DOMESTICATED 3000 B.C.
TO U.S. 1856
WENT WILD IN DESERT SOUTHWEST

HOUSE CAT
DOMESTICATED 8500 B.C.
TO U.S. WITH EARLIEST SETTLERS
WILD, BUT ASSOCIATED WITH HUMANS

DOG
DOMESTICATED 14,000 TO 30,000 B.C.
SEMI-DOMESTIC DOGS WERE IN
THE UNITED STATES FOR CENTURIES;
EUROPEANS BROUGHT MANY
NEW BREEDS FROM 1521 ONWARD

ROCK PIGEON
DOMESTICATED 8000 B.C.
TO U.S. WITH EARLIEST SETTLERS
WILD, BUT ASSOCIATED WITH HUMAN
STRUCTURES

GOAT
DOMESTICATED 8000 B.C.
TO U.S. 1565
WILD IN HAWAII ONLY

SHEEP

DOMESTICATED 8500 B.C.
TO U.S. 1565
WILD IN HAWAII ONLY

GOOSE
DOMESTICATED 1500 B.C.
TO U.S. WITH EARLIEST SETTLERS
ONLY GRAYLAGS GO WILD

DUCK
DOMESTICATED 2500 B.C.
TO U.S. WITH EARLIEST SETTLERS
HYBRIDS WITH MALLARDS GO WILD BRIEFLY

EUROPEAN RABBITS
DOMESTICATED 100 A.D.
TO U.S. WITH EARLIEST SETTLERS
CANNOT COMPETE WITH NATIVE RABBITS;
DO NOT SURVIVE IN THE WILD

TURKEYS
DOMESTICATED 100 B.C.
TO JAMESTOWN, 1607
CANNOT COMPETE WITH NATIVE WILD
TURKEYS;
DO NOT SURVIVE IN THE WILD

Definition of Terms

Feral vs. Wild

Animal scientists refer to domestic animals that escape as being "feral" rather than "wild". After an undefined amount of time the feral species may finally be referred to as wild but the distinction is often not clear.

In this book the term feral will not be used, simply to avoid confusion. Domestic animals are more wild than tame. With few exceptions, they need to be fenced in to keep them from running away. Once loose, they are reluctant to return – no matter how comfortable their life with humans may have been.

Wild Type

Something happens to domestic animals when they return to the wild. If they are wild for more than a few generations, nearly every species, except the lowly burro, makes a physical transformation. After several generations in the wild some typical changes occur. The wild animal generally becomes smaller than the original animal. This is a response to the more difficult conditions and reflects a need to use energy more efficiently. The wild animal can thrive on less food and water per day than it could in captivity. The wild animal (except the donkey) adopts a more streamlined shape and its colors revert back to more basic blacks, browns and grays. Other physical changes occur, such as a longer tail for swatting flies. The wild animal's senses become more acute and it is more sure-footed. The wild animal uses the least amount of motion to accomplish any task.

The changes that occur are limited by the genetic potential of the domestic animal. For example, a domesticated cow that escapes to the wild does not become a horse. But within the boundaries of being the same species, the population of the escaped animals becomes the "wild type" in a few short generations through natural selection and the survival of the fittest. The domestic animal in the wild must become a lean, mean survival machine.

Open Range Ranching

In the early years of European settlement of North and South America there was a shortage of labor. Farm animals were allowed to roam relatively freely without fences. Salt blocks were sometimes used to keep the farm animals close to home. If possible, the farm animals were run in valleys, islands or parcels of land that were blocked off by rivers so they could not escape. Fences were too expensive and labor-intensive to maintain. Roundups were conducted once or twice a year in hopes of finding most of the animals.

If you were a farm animal that was naturally more wild than tame, what would you do? Find the first road out of town. Open Range ranching allowed the escape of farm animals and the establishment of large populations of wild versions of farm animals in North and South America.

Cracker

This word has taken on some relatively negative connotations recently. In this book it simply refers to a Florida cowboy or the farm animals that he tended – for example the Cracker Cow and the Cracker Horse are wild breeds that developed in Florida. The name was first used as a term of respect for the animals and the cowboys who hunted them.

Dominica

The early name for the present-day island of the Dominican Republic and Haiti. Now called Hispaniola. This was the location of the first Spanish settlement in the Western Hemisphere and the place where domesticated animals were first introduced. Wild farm animals thrived in the habitat of Dominica. So much so that the offspring of the Dominican herds provided the seed stock for nearly all of the Spanish introductions into North and South America.

Mustang

The wild horses of the American West. There are two distinct types of Mustangs. *Spanish Mustangs* are pure descendents of the introduced Spanish horses that lived for over 300 years in the wild, subject to natural selection and survival of the fittest. These were the original wild horses that provided transportation and horse power to the early settlers of the American West. Before the Spanish Mustangs, Plains Indians did not have horses. Indians adopted the Spanish Mustangs and, through selective breeding, developed the *Indian Pony*.

The second kind of mustang is any horse that is running wild in the Western United States. In the past 100 years, many breeds of horses have escaped or been released out west. Pure *Spanish Mustangs* have become nearly extinct.

Criollo

A Spanish animal, be it horse, cow or donkey, that lives in North or South American and is slightly changed from the original import.

CHAPTER ONE – HOLY COW! THEY'RE EVERYWHERE. CATTLE INVADE AMERICA.

Cattle introduced to the New World; cattle escaped; population of wild cattle exploded in West Indies; cattle taken to Florida where they established wild populations; new breeds of cattle were formed by natural selection; the cattle culture of Florida; large populations of wild cattle roamed across Virginia; wild cattle in New England contributed to Indian conflicts; wild cattle of the Carolinas and throughout the South.

THE FIRST STOP - DOMINICA, CUBA, JAMAICA AND PUERTO RICO

Europeans brought domestic animals to the Americas as an integral part of their strategy to settle the continents. Their methods of agriculture were transplanted to the Americas to allow their concept of civilization to take root. The importance of farm animals was shown when Columbus brought numerous farm animals on his *second voyage – the first attempt at a permanent settlement.* All subsequent attempts at a permanent settlement in the New World by Spanish, English, French and Dutch settlers included farm animals.

The European settlers came from a more technologically advanced civilization than the one they found in the Americas. Domestication and production of farm animals had been common in Europe for centuries. Efficient agricultural production was the foundation that led to other technological advances, including advances in warfare that gave the Europeans an unstoppable advantage over the indigenous peoples, whose civilizations were among the least technologically advanced of any in the world at the time. (1)

The first settlement in the West Indies, named Isabella, was established by Christopher Columbus west of present-day Puerto Plata, Dominican Republic, near the Bahabonico River. Columbus brought horses, cattle, sheep, swine, goats and chickens to this settlement in 1494. Columbus and his crew were unaware that the animals they were unloading on Dominica were unique to the New World. The Spanish were soon to find that there were no domestic farm animals in the land that would be the United States. Present-day Canada had semi-domestic reindeer; Mexico had domestic turkeys; and there were domesticated llamas, guinea pigs and Muscovy ducks in parts of South America.

Cattle and swine thrived in the environment around the Spanish settlement of Isabella. The native vegetation provided more than enough nourishment for the original numbers of cattle and swine to multiply many times over. Animals were allowed to roam freely without fencing because the settlers lacked the manpower or resources to contain them. This type of Open Range ranching had historically been practiced in parts of Spain and suited the harsh conditions that faced the early Spanish settlers. Open Range ranching is the least labor-intensive method of ranching and was adopted in all of the New World areas until the population of settlers reached a level that allowed more intensive agriculture and fencing. Inevitably, many open range cattle, swine and horses managed to escape to the wild. Farm animals often avoided capture during annual or semi-annual roundups.

The town of Isabella was abandoned in 1498 due to conflicts with native inhabitants, disease, dissension among the Spaniards and a lack of gold near the town. A new settlement was established at the site of present-day Santo Domingo, Dominican Republic. The countryside around Santo Domingo was even more favorable to animals that escaped to the wild. As more settlements were established, wild farm animals became common in all corners of the island.

The following summarizes the extent to which domesticated animals from Spain and the Canary Islands took over the Dominican Republic/Haiti and later Cuba, Jamaica and Puerto Rico:

"*Spanish livestock of all kinds accompanied the initial colonization of the four islands, but with very different results. Sheep and goats did not thrive nearly so well in the new environment, perhaps partly for climatic reasons, but horses prospered and both cattle and swine attained an almost outrageous success. Pigs took to the abundant forests as if to a native habitat, easily crowding out a variety of small indigenous mammals to occupy a largely uncontested ecological niche....Criollo (Spanish) cattle achieved a parallel preadapted success on the savannas, attaining almost at once a prodigious rate of reproduction at nearly their biological potential. Longhorn herds reputedly increased tenfold in less than half a decade, quite possible assuming that heifers formed most of the imported stock. In the short run, they encountered no competing large herbivores, suffered no diseases or parasites, and faced no predators in these bovine Elysian Fields. The island Indians had made little use of the savannas, leaving them open to the invading cattle, and the incredible mortality rate among the (Indian) tribes quickly created grassy old fields, extending the cattle range....Eventually European dogs gone feral filled the vacant predator niche in the islands, especially the Dominican Republic/Haiti, controlling the herds and droves, but the initial proliferation of cattle and swine can only be described as astounding."* (2)

There were vast areas of unsettled land in Mexico, the United States and the Islands of the West Indies for several hundred years after Spain claimed them as part of the Spanish Empire. Escaped domestic animals had all of this free land to themselves, with few predators. Thus, the population of escaped farm animals often exceeded the number of farm animals under the supervision of the settlers in those areas. (3)

During the early and mid-1500's, the islands of Dominica, Cuba, Jamaica and Puerto Rico became home to wild herds of cattle that were more common than any other large animal on the island, save that other farm animal – wild swine.

The cattle that became wild on the four islands were from the Andalusian region of Spain and the Canary Islands and were thought to remain the pure Spanish type. The cattle were of many colors, but a similar type. Many of the modern-day cattle breeds had not yet been developed. The Spanish cattle of these early days were black, roan, reddish-brown, and white with black marks on the neck or ears, spotted and speckled with long horns. (4)

John Rouse, in his book *The Criollo,* attempts to describe the Spanish type cattle. There are no pictures or written descriptions of the original cattle that were brought to the United States. Instead, Rouse postulates that there is nothing in the history of Andalusian cattle to indicate that they have changed greatly over the years. There are three broad groupings of old Spanish cattle now in Andalusia (and Criollo cattle in the New World bear many similarities to these types):

Red: The *Retinto,* a red- to tan-colored animal sometimes almost brown.
Black: The *Black Andalusian,* a solid black.
White: The *Berrenda,* always with black markings; and the all-white *Cacereno.* Both white breeds were native to Estemadura which borders Andalusia on the Northwest. (5)

The Retinto color is typically solid over the entire body and varies in different herds from a Jersey-tan to a bright cherry red...Any white on the Retinto is frowned on, but the extremities are usually of a lighter shade. The horns on the cow are rather thin, very wide, up spread and frequently have lyre-shaped ends. On the bull the horns usually are much thicker and shorter, but on some individuals widespread horns upturned at the ends are seen. The head is long and narrow. Conformation, while indicative of a beef type, is inclined to be rather rough. The legs are large boned, and the body stands well off the ground. Top and bottom lines are quite parallel; there is little tendency for the bottom line to cut up at the flank (Note: this seems to be a constant characteristic of descendents of Spanish cattle). The barrel is well rounded but not particularly deep.
The Berrenda has a predominantly white body commonly marked with minor black spots around the shoulders and on the neck. Occasionally solid black spots are seen. The ears are invariably black or red.....The Berrenda is quite similar to the Retinto in general conformation (shape)... ... The Cacereno does not have black spots on the body or black ears.

The Black Andalusians....are solid black animals. The horns on the cow are widespread and upturned , not as large as on the Retinto but of the same typical shape as most Spanish cattle....the rather thin face, prominent tail stock and the thin dewlap are characteristic. (From pp. 18, 19, 216-224 of Rouse, 1977) (Note: many of the wild black cattle on Hawaii were near carbon-copies of the Black Andalusians).

Large cattle herds quickly became an economic benefit to the islands much as they later became an economic force in America. The island cattle were not driven to market like the ones in Florida and the West, so a similar cowboy culture did not develop. Instead, herds of cattle on the islands were allowed to flourish on their own, unfenced, and were rounded up every so often to harvest their hides. The cattle had no value as meat because an over-abundance of meat was available to the small Spanish population on the islands and meat could not be sent back to Spain economically. The hides, however, soon became more important than the elusive gold for export to Europe. (6)

Open Range ranching often is an invitation for cattle rustlers. Once the word got out that there was a large population of valuable wild cattle on the islands, largely unguarded, it was only natural for someone to try to steal them. That someone turned out to be the pirates of the Caribbean.

French pirates of the early 1600's had a home base on the north shore of present-day Haiti. This part of the island had no Spanish settlers and an abundance of easily-obtained food – the wild cattle and swine. In addition to normal pirate activities, these pirates found that the hides of the wild cattle were valuable. The pirates collected and sold cattle hides. They also dried and smoked the meat, called "boucans". The term buccaneer is derived from the name of this popular French pirate fare. The name buccaneer became synonymous with pirate in 1684 when Alexandre Exquemelin's book *The Buccaneers of America* was published. (7)

One small island's name suggests how common the wild cattle had become – Cow Island. The notorious pirate, Captain Henry Morgan, used Cow Island as a rendezvous point for one of his most infamous raids. In 1668, at Cow Island, he commandeered the French pirate ship *Le Cerf Volant* which had been used by the French cattle hunters of Haiti. Re-named *The Satisfaction,* this was Captain Morgan's flagship for his assault on Panama City. (8)

When some of the small Spanish population moved to the United States to search for gold, French settlers and retired pirates filled the void on that side of the island. Eventually, the French settled the northwest corner of Hispaniola and Haiti became a French colony.

Wild cattle roamed the islands of Dominica, Cuba, Jamaica and Puerto Rico from 1495 to 1700. 50 generations of cattle were born free and lived in the mountains of the islands without ever seeing a human. There were so many wild cattle on the islands that it became a sport to hunt them in a manner similar to hunting any other large mammal. Such a hunt was not without danger to the hunter as a wild bull could weigh over 1500 pounds and become fierce when cornered or chased.

The original Spanish cattle have since been crossed with Brahmas and other modern breeds in large cattle holdings so it is unlikely that any of the current island cattle remain true to the wild population. However, in small holdings and subsistence farms there are cattle that still remain very similar to the Andalusian source cattle. (9)

FLORIDA - WILD CATTLE HERDS 100 YEARS BEFORE PLYMOUTH ROCK

Florida was the first stop for cattle on the mainland of the United States. In 1521, Juan Ponce de Leon made his second trip to Florida attempting to establish a Spanish colony. Spanish settlers always brought horses, cattle and other domestic animals. The horses were for transportation, plowing the land and for use in battle. The other domestic animals were seed stock for herds that would hopefully grow large enough to provide food for the future colony.

According to some historians, the Ponce de Leon trip of 1521 was the first introduction of domestic animals to the United States. (10) Ponce de Leon's delegation was routed by native warriors and forced to retreat to Cuba. There is no record of the fate of the cattle that landed in Florida in 1521. It is possible that they escaped and established a presence in the wild.

The next Spanish exploration of Florida occurred in 1527, led by Pamfilo de Narvaez. Spanish conquistadors normally took horses for combat and cattle and hogs for rations. It is not known if Narvaez took any cattle to Florida – the historical record does not explicitly say that he did. His excursion to Florida went very poorly and it is assumed that any cattle that may have accompanied the army did not survive. (11)

In 1539, Hernando de Soto led the ultimate quest into Florida. The historic record is clear that cattle were introduced to Florida during his expedition. de Soto's army was in Florida and the Southern United States for three and a half years – from May, 1539 to late 1542. They explored present-day Florida, most of the southeastern states, Arkansas, Oklahoma and the Mississippi river before abandoning the search for gold. Midway through the expedition, in 1540, Diego Maldonado planned to rendezvous with de Soto near present-day Pensacola, Florida to re-supply the expedition. The rendezvous did not occur and Maldonado left a sizeable herd of cattle in Florida when he left. (12) Again, there is no way to know if any of these cattle survived in the wild, but there is every possibility that they did, since the environment and vegetation were conducive to survival.

In 1565, Pedro Menendez de Aviles established the first permanent Spanish settlements in St. Augustine, Florida. As these settlements grew, more cattle were introduced, mainly from Cuba. By the early 1600's significant numbers of wild cattle existed in most parts of Florida. Catholic missions were established from 1600 to 1680 in northern Florida. The missions taught cattle production to natives as a way to assimilate them into Spanish culture. The Seminole Indians readily took to raising cattle in the Open Range system and prospered from it, along with the Spanish rancheros. From 1705 to 1850, the Seminole Indians were large holders of cattle in Florida. (13)

Florida remained sparsely populated until after 1821, when it became a U.S. territory. From 1565 to about 1850 there was plenty of empty space in Florida for wild cattle to thrive and multiply. For approximately 80 generations, cattle were subject to the laws of natural selection and survival of the fittest in Florida. They had to withstand heat, an abundance of rain, sometime droughts, wild cats, alligators, bears, mosquitoes and tropical diseases. From this came a breed that is still recognized today – the Florida Cracker cow. Florida Cracker cattle eventually became a prominent economic factor in the growth of the state, much as the Texas Longhorn was important to the growth of the Western frontier. They are smaller than the Longhorn, with cows in good condition weighting from 600-800 pounds. Their horns are smaller than the Longhorns and have a tendency to curve upward rather than outward. They have been noted for their longevity and reproductive vigor. (14)

The first Spanish cattle were thought to be solid black, solid reddish-brown or solid white in color. (15) Florida Cracker cattle are sometimes spotted or roan, suggesting that they became mixed with English breeds in the 18th or 19th century.

When Florida became a United States territory in 1821, large numbers of homesteaders invaded the state from the north, to settle on property they owned or property that nobody owned. The only possessions of some of the homesteaders were a few captured Florida Cracker cattle. (16)

Due to the abundance of wild cattle, the new territory of Florida soon became a source of cattle for processors in the United States. Cattle were driven from Central Florida to ports on the Gulf Coast, to the Panhandle of Florida and to markets in South Carolina and Georgia. The Florida trail drives were shorter in distance than the trail drives from West Texas to Abilene, Kansas, but they had many of the same problems – swollen streams, stampedes, Indian raids, lost dogies and difficult weather.

The profits from sales of cattle helped establish Florida as an economically viable territory, soon to be a state. Unfortunately, conflicts between the rancheros and the Seminoles over ownership of free-roaming cattle helped precipitate the series of Seminole Wars. These wars ultimately resulted in relocation of the Seminole tribes to Oklahoma. (17)

THE COWBOY CULTURE OF FLORIDA

From about 1850 to 1890, Florida developed towns, open range ranches and a cowboy culture. There wasn't much to distinguish Florida from the Wild West, except the climate and the topography. Florida had cowboys, Indians, gunfights, rustlers, vigilantes, trail rides (although shorter), horse thieves, roundups, bulldogging, barroom brawls, colorful characters, bad food, low wages and cattle barons -- all built on the economic potential of the Florida Cracker cattle.

Here are a few cowboy stories from *Florida Cowman, A History of Florida Cattle Raising* by Joe A. Akerman (1976) which capture the flavor of that brief period of Florida history:

The next time you are at Walt Disney World in Orlando/Kissimmee, be sure to remember this tidbit:

p. 152. Another lively cow town during this period was Kissimmee. The first bars in America established to accommodate mounted customers (drive- thrus) were built here for cowmen about 1870. This was a decade before they began to appear in the West. Cowmen simply rode up to these outside refreshment stands and ordered their poison – whether it be corn whiskey, peach spirits, rot-gut or can skimming whiskey.

A Florida Stampede:

p. 181 I never will forget one big stampede I saw at Fort Basinger. Eleven hundred steers went into a stampede. We men heard it in time and run in every direction. The stampede headed for a big swamp. Wasn't a thing we could do. The next morning we followed the trail down to the edge of the swamp. We knowed that the ground was too soft for 'em to get across. They didn't, but you couldn't see no cows at all. All you could see was horns – just a whole lake of horns.

The cattle caught during a roundup normally belonged to more than one ranchero. Often, five or six rancheros had their cattle run on the same Open Range. The cows were marked with ear tags or brands, but the calves were not yet. It was commonly understood that any calves belonged to the owner of the cow that belonged with the calf. Getting the cow and calf matched up after the confusion of the roundup and penning required the art of "mammying-up":

p. 186 Oh there is ways to do that. Don't care how many you got the same color, there is a difference between 'em if you know how to look. All I need to do is to pen 'em for one day and the next day I can tell you which is which. Supposing you had twenty red calves to mammy-up. If you look at 'em good, one's color is just a teeny bit different. One is got a different set around the shoulder. The hair is curled in a peculiar way on a front leg, maybe, and so on and so forth. Things like that will tell you. You can't depend on the calf. He will mammy-up with any cow. Then, too, I think hard about it, and some of them calves come before me in my sleep. It is something you have to get straight, else you'll get the wrong marking brand on 'em. Some breeders who can't do it themselves will get me to do it for 'em, and then set up on the corral fence and wonder can I do it. I always tell 'em, ten dollars for any mistake I make.

THE FLORIDA LEGEND, BONE MIZELL

Bone Mizell was the most widely celebrated of the Cracker Cowboys. He lived his life on the Palmetto prairie and excelled at all of the jobs of a Cracker Cowboy, including the most unpleasant tasks or the jobs requiring the greatest skill. He was born into a relatively prominent family, but took on the cowboy life as an adult. For long periods of time, Bone Mizell had no house or home. He lived and slept on the prairie, working for one ranchero or another. Or skimming the "extra" wild, unclaimed cattle from the plentiful herds and selling them as his own.

In addition to being a real Cracker Cowboy, Bone had a ready story for anyone who would listen. He was the Will Rogers of Florida. Or, as some would have it, Will Rogers was the Bone Mizell of Oklahoma.

Some of the stories about Bone Mizell may have been taken from other sources and attributed to Bone. Some of the stories may have been exaggerated in the same manner that Bone Mizell would have done. The fact that the stories were attributed to Bone throughout the state of Florida attests to his popularity at the time. **See Appendix One for selected stories about Bone Mizell.**

VIRGINIA TIDEWATER - A NATURAL HOME FOR CATTLE

Sir Richard Grenville brought the first cattle to the Roanoke Colony of Virginia in 1585. At the time, it was much less expensive to pick up livestock from Dominica than to bring them from Britain by ship -- livestock had a better chance of survival on the short trip from Dominica to Virginia. By the time of Grenville's visit in 1585, wild cattle had multiplied many times over on Dominica. The Spaniards were happy to sell the surplus. Grenville was able to purchase livestock even though Spain and Britain were officially hostile at the time. The Spanish authorities on Dominica were already becoming independent of Spain because of the lack of timely communication and the need to look out for their own economic well-being. Grenville enjoyed a wild cattle hunt while a guest of the Spanish authorities. (18)

There is no record that the livestock of the original Roanoke Colony survived. Some may have escaped and survived in the wild to begin the process of building a wild population in Virginia. It is certain that the people did not survive and the colony was mysteriously lost. (19)

The first successful British settlement in Virginia was Jamestown, founded in 1607. These settlers brought domestic animals on the first expedition and were re-supplied several times. However, most of these animals were eaten by the settlers to avoid starvation in the winter of 1609-1610. When some of the animals were eaten, it was impossible to increase the herds to a sustainable level. The colony could not grow without farm animals. (20)

In 1611 Sir Thomas Dale brought more livestock to the Jamestown settlement. In order to insure that they would multiply to provide food for the future of the settlement, he decreed that no domestic livestock could be killed by anyone without the consent of the governor -- on pain of death. The threat of capital punishment for eating a cow or pig helped insure the survival of the Jamestown colony. (21)

Spanish cattle from Dominica were some of the first cattle brought to Virginia. Soon, the favored types of English cattle were brought by individual settlers. New emigrants brought cattle from their home regions. English cattle became the most common type in Virginia. Livestock increased slowly in the Tidewater area.

The settlers intended to establish English-style farming in the new world. They intended to establish small farms with fenced-in cattle, swine and other livestock and grow crops similar to the ones in Britain. The reality of pioneer conditions forced the settlers to spend most of their time clearing land and trying to get any English crops to grow in the sandy soil of the Tidewater. The settlers soon found that the only crop that would be economically viable was tobacco. During the early to mid 1600's tobacco became the commodity that allowed the colonies of Virginia and Maryland to succeed.

The tobacco farmers attempted to maintain an Open Range supply of cattle, but could not afford the time or resources to monitor the cattle closely. Before long, there were more cattle in the wild of Virginia than were closely held by the farmers. The winters were mild and there were abundant open grasslands, swamps and forested land – an ideal habitat for wild cattle.

Wild cattle and swine became a threat to the all-important tobacco industry by trampling the fields. It was impractical to try to fence in the livestock. Instead, the colony required the tobacco farmers to fence in their crop. In 1643, the Virginia House of Burgesses passed a law requiring colonists to fence their tobacco and other crops in order to protect their most valuable commodity. The height and style of the fence was specified. Maryland later passed a similar law. (22)

Virginia was settled relatively quickly, so wild cattle were subdued after a few decades.

NEW ENGLAND AND THE NORTHEAST – CATTLE AND INDIAN TROUBLES

Cattle were introduced to New England just a few years after they were successful in Virginia. The Mayflower did not bring any domestic animals (except two dogs) on the voyage of 1620. The first cattle were brought over in 1624. The Massachusetts Bay Company brought thousands of domestic animals to New England during the 1630's. By

1650, the cattle population of New England was growing at a slow and steady pace. In a similar manner, the Dutch West India Company supplied cattle to the settlements in present-day New York. (23)

Cattle-raising was considered a civilized pursuit by Englishmen of the time. They had refined various techniques and took pride in their system of husbandry. In England, cattle were raised in permanent fenced pastures, there were some improvements in breeds through selective breeding, most bulls were neutered and only the best bulls were allowed to breed. The typical English farmer spent hours each day caring for his herd. (24)

The New England settlers envisioned a similar type of husbandry in their new home. The native vegetation and topography of New England was ideal for transplanting the English system of farming to the new world. However, the unexpected amount of work involved in clearing land, establishing a homestead, fighting the weather and establishing profitable crops overwhelmed the English settlers early on. Despite the best of intentions, the New England cattle were allowed to roam in the Open Range system until a more "English" system could be afforded. As in every other frontier, some of the cattle escaped to the wild and thrived in their new surroundings.

The New England wild herds of cattle did not grow to the size of the ones in Florida, Virginia and the Western frontier. Several factors worked against the wild cattle herds of New England. First, of course, were the winters. The cattle that did escape had a lower survival rate, but many were able to deal with the northern winters. Second, the English farmers neutered any male calf that was not destined to be a breeding bull. Third, colonization of the Northeastern United States proceeded fairly quickly after the initial settlements and the advancing settlers either captured the wild cattle or forced them to move further west. And fourth, the New England farmers found various nooks, valleys or islands to pasture their cattle. The topography of the Northeast allowed Open Range cattle to be somewhat contained. Still, some bulls or pregnant cows escaped. The wild herd became self-sustaining for many years.

Wild cattle never became an economic force in New England or the Northeast. There were no organized roundups of wild cattle and no cowboy culture came about.

The wild cattle were mainly a nuisance to the farmers. On more than a few occasions, a wild bull was reported to steal away a cow or two from the domestic herd. One such account was given in early New England of a domestic herd that was "molested by reason of several heards of wilde cattle resorting among their tame". (25)

Wild cattle were plentiful enough to contribute to the aggravation between the settlers and the natives. Indian tribes had hunted and lived in the region for centuries and some of the land was considered to be sacred by the Indians. However, the settlers saw abundant unoccupied land. In legal terms, the English felt that any undeveloped land was available for settlement. An Englishman, Robert Gray, said of the Virginia territory, "Savages have no particular proprietie in any part or parcell of that Country, but only a general recidencie there, as wild beasts have in the forest." (26)

As Englishmen moved further inland, wild cattle and tame cattle were free to move about. These cattle often wandered into Indian settlements, destroying crops and housing. Indians killed cattle as they would any other wild animal that posed a threat to their crops, even though some of the cattle were owned by the English settlers. These conflicts played out in much the same fashion as the Florida conflicts and later conflicts in the Great Plains.

The following description of these conflicts is condensed from pp. 232-237 of *Creatures of Empire* (Anderson, 2004):

In 1641 various conflicts between natives and English settlers in New England caused the Narragansett chief, Miantonomi, to attempt to organize a pan-Indian resistance. Until that time the Indian tribes were split into warring factions that did not agree on the best response to the intruding English. Much of Miantonomi's argument for the unity of Indian resistance spoke of the intrusion of wild farm animals. Speaking to other tribes and asking that they join the resistance, Miantonomi said:

"You know our fathers had plenty of deer and skins, our plains were full of deer, as also our woods, and of turkies, and our coves full of fish and fowl. But these English having gotten our land, they with scythes cut down the grass, and with axes fell the trees; their cows and horses eat the grass, and their hogs spoil our clam banks, and we shall all be starved: therefore it is best for you to do as we." (27)

"That animals could help to incite a war between human combatants was eminently clear to New Englanders by the early 1670's (30 years after Miantonomi's warning). Angry Massachusetts colonists in a newly settled part of Dedham nearly attacked Wampanoag Indians in the spring of 1671 over a trespass dispute. English families had recently driven the Wampanoags from the area, and displaced Indians apparently took their revenge on roaming livestock. Urging forbearance from the Dedham settlers, the Bay Colony's Indian superintendent, Daniel Gookin, pleaded that it was not worth *'fighting with Indians about horses and hogs, as matters too low to shed blood'*. If the colonists would keep their animals on their own land, Gookin advised, similar losses could be avoided and peace preserved." (28)

What was to become known as King Philips War had its origin partly in these kinds of animal disputes.

"Within months, the Narragansetts joined in the fighting against the colonists, entering the kind of pan-Indian alliance that their former chief, Miantonomi, had once advocated. But instead of sparing livestock until deer populations rebounded, as Miantonomi had suggested, this new generation of Indians made English animals special targets of their wrath.....By November, 1675, Connecticut magistrates worried so much about livestock losses that they advised inhabitants to *'kill and salt up what of their cattell were fit to kill'* lest the Indians take them first." (29)

The King Philips War was estimated to cost 3,000 English and 7,000 Indian lives, 1,200 houses destroyed and 8,000 cattle killed along with immeasurable losses to Indian property. (30)

As New England and the Northeast became fully settled, wild cattle were eventually eliminated. Wild cattle never gained a foothold as the frontier moved into the Midwestern states.

SOUTH CAROLINA - CATTLE CAPITAL OF THE COLONIES

As the Colonies grew, each one specialized in its most promising economic pursuit. South Carolina and coastal Georgia became the cattle capital of the Colonies due to its favorable climate and lush vegetation. Large stocks of cattle were held by private ranchers as early as 1680. The cattle came from other colonies, Bermuda and England itself. They were basic English cattle – the modern English breeds had not yet been developed. (31)

Carolina cattle were tended in the Open Range system, but they were watched more closely than the Florida cattle. The human population of South Carolina had grown rapidly. Escaped cattle did not find large areas of unpopulated land in South Carolina. Too, the Carolina ranchers used salt blocks effectively as a control tool for their herds. The availability of salt blocks tended to keep Open Range cattle within a reasonable distance for roundups. The main influence of wild cattle was felt when a wild bull would lure cows away from the main herd. To combat this, male calves were captured and castrated on a regular schedule. Also, a South Carolina law required that a certain number of cowboys be assigned to each herd of cattle to maintain control.

Eventually, Carolina ranchers needed more land for their domestic cattle herds. Some Carolinians expanded their operations to Florida. Some brought English breeds to Florida where they probably mixed with the Spanish cattle to influence the Florida Cracker breed.

In the early years of cattle production in South Carolina and coastal Georgia, cattle were often run on barrier islands. This insured that the cattle could not escape. As the island operations became too small to remain profitable, the livestock were often abandoned and lived wild on the islands for many decades. One such island – Green Island, Georgia – was used as a hunting club. **See Appendix Two for a detailed story about wild cattle hunting on Green Island.**

South Carolina remained a strong cattle producing state until the frontier moved west. (32)

CATTLE MOVE WEST WITH THE FRONTIER

As the frontier moved west, cattle ranching moved with it. Many South Carolina cattlemen moved into Georgia and Alabama where land was cheaper and space was not limited. Eventually, more modern breeds of cattle were imported and the wild cattle to be found throughout the South became a mix of many breeds, rather than the pure Spanish or English type. These mixes eventually found their way to Louisiana and on to Texas where they played a part in the genetics of the Longhorn breed. (33)

Georgia, Alabama and Mississippi produced a breed of cattle similar to the Florida Cracker Cow. Called Pineywood Cattle, the breed came from the early introductions of Spanish cattle. Some may have come from the cattle Maldonado abandoned near Pensacola, Florida.

The Pineywoods breed was shaped by agricultural and environmental conditions in the southeastern United States. This, along with some human selection, has resulted in a breed that is heat tolerant, long-lived, resistant to parasites and diseases, and able to be productive on marginal forage

A small number of Pineywoods cattle remain in private herds today. (34)

WILD CATTLE IN THE SOUTH - UNCLE REMUS STORIES

Joel Chandler Harris wrote the *Tales of Uncle Remus*, published beginning in 1880. *The Tales of Uncle Remus* were told through the lives of the wild animals that lived in the Southern U.S. at the time – the rabbit, the fox, the bear, the turtle, the wildcat, etc. It was natural for Mr. Harris to include wild cattle in his stories as they were a part of the fauna of the South at the time.   Three of the Uncle Remus tales were about Wild Cows and their relations with the other animals of the woods. (35)

LOUISIANA – FRENCH CATTLE BREEDS, MARSHLAND SWAMPERS

A significant cattle industry developed in Louisiana by 1765. The cattle came from Mexico, the Carolinas, Florida and perhaps other sources. Early French settlers brought cattle from French Canada. This mixture of breeds found their way into Eastern Texas in the early 1800's and probably contributed to some degree to the background of the Texas Longhorn.

Cattle that escaped from Louisiana ranches flourished in the wilder parts of Southern Louisiana. No special breed developed in the wild of Louisiana, but some of them did attract a name: Swampers.

"Many drifted into marshes, obtaining all the salt they needed simply by grazing, thereby rendering useless the Carolinian herd-control device of salting. These 'swampers' became almost fully wild. All things considered, the subtropical, moist coastal prairies offered a splendid natural setting for cattle, one in which they could have thrived without human interference." (36)

WILD CATTLE FROM COAST TO COAST

Remarkably, there were no farm animals in California until 250 years after they were introduced to the Eastern United States. Spain made minimal efforts to colonize California because of its great distance from Mexico City. Finally in 1769 Father Junipero Serra established the first Catholic Mission in San Diego. Horses, cattle and other farm animals were brought to the mission. In the next 50 years, 20 other missions were established along the coast of California. (37) Within a few decades, there was a surplus of cattle, mostly wild, from San Diego to San Francisco. The hills and valleys of coastal California presented the most ideal climate for wild cattle to increase than any other place in the New World. Open Range ranching was practiced by the Spanish missions. Private ownership of ranches expanded after 1800 and they also practiced Open Range ranching. Privately-owned herds mixed with wild herds and the annual roundups seldom distinguished between the two. There were plenty of cattle to go around. In fact, many Californians did not "own" any cattle. When they needed beef, they simply went to the hills and brought some home. Cattle seemed to be as numerous as the fishes in the sea and they were considered everyone's property for many years in the early, congenial era of California history. (38)

The population of California remained very low in the years of the Spanish missions. In fact, the entire state had only 6,000 Spaniards by 1841 – 72 years after the first mission. Free from interference by Spain and Mexico, "California at this period was idyllically pastoral, a paradise of beauty and abundance. The seeds and cuttings brought in by the missionary priests had multiplied into a cornucopian plenty." (39) Adding to the spirit of tranquility, the California Indians were much less aggressive than Eastern and Plains Indians. For example, when Spanish horses were brought to California, many of the Indians continued to live as they had for centuries, finding no need for the new mode of transportation.

The cattle of early California were the pure Spanish type, brought from Mexico. No other breeds were introduced until some cattle were driven from Texas in the mid-1800's. The Transcontinental Railroad brought improved breeds of cattle after 1868.

Spanish cattle from California were taken to Hawaii and Australia by George Vancouver in 1793. Years later, the wild cattle of Hawaii remained very similar to pictures of wild Spanish cattle in California. (40)

The Gold Rush of 1849 created such a demand for beef that nearly all of the wild cattle in the state were depleted in a few years. There were hundreds of cattle drives from Southern California to the gold fields. Because of these cattle drives, the California Cowboy became part of the state's early history.

Soon after the Gold Rush, the California ranches had adequate manpower to bring the range under control. Mixing with Texas Longhorns and modern cattle breeds brought the end of the pure Spanish cattle that had contributed to the history of Spanish Colonial California. (41)

Despite its short duration, the period of wild cattle in California spawned a cowboy culture in the state. Stories are handed down about the thrilling hunts and cattle drives to the gold fields. When the western movie became a staple of Hollywood, movie companies didn't have to look far to find real cowboys. And the place names scattered throughout the state leave no doubt about the creatures that once roamed free: Wild Cattle Creek near Monterey, Wild Cattle Mountain east of Redding and Wild Cattle Canyon near Salt Point State Park, for example.

WHAT CATTLE BREEDS WENT WILD IN THE UNITED STATES?

Breed registries and modern selective breeding of cattle did not exist at the time of introduction of cattle into the United States.

Emigrants to the United States normally brought their best livestock with them. Records indicate that cattle normally came from the same locale as the settlers. But the cattle were not described by a breed name. Rather, the cattle came from "Lancashire", "York", "Northumberland" or "Andalusia".

Photographs or detailed descriptions of colors and types of cattle of the time do not exist. Because of the difficult circumstances of pioneer life, maintaining the quality of the introduced cattle was nearly impossible.

Since the early cattle were not fixed breeds with predictable characteristics and offspring, the mixing of cattle in the new world brought even more diversity in type. Cattle in the wild became a vast mixture of colors and type.

Until the 1860's the cattle in the United States were generally a hodge-podge of types:

"The result of all these indefinite and purposeless intermixtures of breed is now daily seen in herds which are brought into our eastern markets....they are of all possible shapes, colors and character, from the very worst to tolerably good, except in those districts where "improved" blood has been introduced, and better care in breeding and keeping has been practiced." (42)

This non-descript mixture of bovines became known simply as "American Cattle" until they were replaced by modern breeds from England, France, Holland and Germany. None of the modern breeds were derived from selections of American Cattle.

The Florida Cracker, the Pineywoods and the Texas Longhorn were fixed breeds that came from natural selection and survival of the fittest in the wild of Florida, the Southeast, Mexico and Texas. They started as pure Spanish types, but later had some mixing with other breeds.

CONTACTS AND PRESERVATION GROUPS

To locate existing herds of Florida Cracker cattle:

1. Florida Department of Agriculture and Consumer Services Division of Animal Industry

2. The Florida Cracker Cattle Association

To locate existing herds of Pineywoods cattle:

1. The Pineywoods Cattle Registry and Breeders Association

CHAPTER TWO – THE TEXAS LONGHORN, THE PINNACLE OF BOVINE FAME

Spanish cattle entered United States from Mexico; Longhorn breed came from 350 years in the wild; millions of Longhorns were wild in the Southwest; how they behaved in the wild; behavior on trail drives; efforts to preserve the breed.

To many, the Texas Longhorn was the most magnificent animal to ever live in the wild in the United States. The longhorn breed came from escaped domestic cattle that moved into the unpopulated areas of Texas and neighboring plains states. These animals adapted and modified through natural selection in the wild. They became a distinct breed in the same manner that the Florida Cracker Cow adapted to the conditions in Florida. Both were descendants of the original Spanish cattle that came from Hispaniola (Dominica), often referred to as Criollo cattle. John E. Rouse describes the stature of the Texas Longhorn this way: "The Criollo cow has been consistently ignored by historians, yet one segment of her progeny, the Longhorn, has been lauded to the pinnacle of bovine fame." (1)

The longhorn was bigger, stronger and more deadly than the native buffalo. A grizzly bear was hardly a match for a mature longhorn bull – a longhorn bull could weigh 1,600 pounds while the average grizzly weighs only 500 pounds. Texas Longhorn cattle dominated tens of millions of acres of the Southern Plains without fear from any natural predators, including the panther and the wolf. Because of its social structure in the wild, a family of longhorns would greet an attack with a flurry of flying hooves, hard and sharp, flying in every direction. (2)

A longhorn ran as fast as a wild mustang. It could run further than the native deer and antelope. The sense of smell of a wild longhorn was as keen as a deer. It could sense a water hole 10 miles away. It thrived on semi-desert plants that were of no use to other animals. It lived in conditions that could not maintain populations of other species. (3)

INTRODUCTION INTO MEXICO AND TEXAS

The ancestors of the longhorns were the first cattle introduced to North America from Dominica, via Andalusia and the Canary Islands. Gregorio de Villalobos took cattle to Mexico in 1521. As in the islands, the new species exploded in numbers in Mexico. The early development of the longhorn breed began in Northern Mexico.

The first longhorns to enter Texas came with the expedition of Francisco Vasquez de Coronado in 1548. It is unlikely that any of his cattle survived to provide seed stock for the Texas Longhorn, but some may have.

Significant numbers of Spanish cattle came into Texas with the establishment of Missions in the late 1600's and early 1700's. It didn't take long for large herds of wild cattle to expand into much of the state. By the time of Texas independence from Mexico in 1836, the Longhorn breed had been developing for 300 years in Mexico and 150 years in Texas – all through natural selection and adaptation to the new environment. (4)

By 1836, estimates of the number of Longhorns running wild in Texas ranged into the millions. By the late 1800's when the Longhorn breed began to decline there were more than 10 million wild Longhorns in Texas, by conservative estimates. (5)

In the early 1800's other breeds of cattle were introduced into Texas by English and German settlers and settlers of other nationalities. Documentation of the number and types of cattle introduced is scant. There is no way to know the extent of mixing between the Spanish Longhorn cattle and other breeds. The most apt description of the resulting mix is from John E. Rouse: "Basically, they were Criollo cattle (Spanish mix) modified by natural selection during 350 years in North America (Mexico and Texas), on which a small degree of crossing with northern European cattle had been imposed for a few decades." (6)

The Longhorn became an economic force due to its large numbers and the growing demand for beef as the population of the United States grew in the mid-1800's. There were so many Longhorns that they were essentially free for anyone who could catch them.

The cost of driving the cattle to market was minimal. A crew of a dozen or fewer cowhands could drive a herd of a few thousand Longhorns 1,000 miles at very low cost per cow. Cowboys were low paid. The attraction to the job of running cattle in Texas was the same as in Florida, California and anywhere else – it was a way of life. (7)

The Texas Longhorn gave rise to the Western cowboy. Without the longhorns, the mystique of the American Cowboy would not have been the same.

PHYSICAL DESCRIPTION OF THE LONGHORN

The Texas Longhorn had all of the common features of Spanish cattle – the head was long and narrow, body standing well off the ground, top line and bottom line parallel, prominent tailstock, thin dewlap and long horns.

The Texas Longhorn was long-legged, enabling it to run well and stand up to trail drives. Some herds actually gained weight during a long drive to market. (8) The Texas Longhorn had a tail that dragged near the ground, apparently an adaptation for swatting flies. The Texas Longhorns were longer in body than most breeds. They were angular and thin when viewed from the front or back -- called "slab sided". They were not fast to put on weight, but could weigh up to 1600 pounds when mature and carry an adequate amount of meat. (9)

Texas Longhorns had widely varying coloration, something that is apparent in photographs and paintings of longhorns on the trail. "It is incorrect to say that they represented all colors of the rainbow. Their colors were more varied than the rainbow, but they were generally dull, earthlike. There were brindles; blues – mulberry blue, ring-streaked blue, speckled blue; *grullas* –so-named because they had the hue of the sand-hill crane, called also mouse-colored, or slate; duns, dark, washed-out and Jersey creams – all hues of yellow; browns with bay points and bays with brown points; blacks, solid and splotched with white, brown and red; whites, both cleanly bright and dirty speckled; many *sabinas* red-and-white peppered; reds of all shades except the dark richness characteristic of Herefords, pale reds being very common; paints of many combinations. The line along the back was common, as in the mustang breed. Coarse brown hairs around the ears were characteristic." (10)

The Longhorn exhibited a sense of color, size, strength and wildness that made it an excellent subject for artists. Of course, placed against the backdrop of the western plains and the excitement of a roundup or trail drive the longhorn was a more interesting subject than ordinary domesticated animals. Frederick Remington and Charlie Russell used Texas Longhorns as subjects of many of their paintings. There are many artists today who are devoted to painting the cowboy life and the Texas Longhorn.

The horns were longer than the original Spanish type, but not as long as fanciful fictions have made them to be. Photographs from the late 1800's show horns from four to six feet wide. Dobie reported that the early cows and steers that were trailed to Kansas had horns from 4 to 5 feet wide. A few notable steers had 6 foot horns. The older (larger) cattle were driven to market first. As the trail drives continued, many of the cattle were captured at a younger age. In the last years of the trail drives, there were few cattle with horns more than 4 feet wide. (11)

Older animals have greater potential for long horns. Horns continue to grow for 12 to 15 years. Genetics, stresses and food sources also play a part in the size of the horns. Horns can be measured from tip to tip or along the length of the horns, following the curve. Tip to tip will give a narrower reading. The two methods of measurement account for some of the discrepancies between measurements of the more famous long horns. There were no horns that measured 13 to 18 feet across, despite such claims in newspapers and circus flyers. Some longhorns in the late 1800's were shown at fairs to show off their prodigious horns. At these fairs, claims of horns from 7 to 8 feet, tip to tip, were the most common.

In more recent years, Texas Longhorns have become a registered breed. There are many private owners who work to preserve the breed. Some of these Longhorns may have been selectively bred for longer horns than those found in the past. There is an annual showcase held by the Texas Longhorn Breeders Association of America. The widest horns from tip to tip at this showcase are in the 8 to 9 foot range. Measured along the curve, they reach 11 to 12 feet. (12)

HOW THEY BEHAVED IN THE WILD

More is known about the Longhorn in the wild than perhaps any other domestic animal gone wild. This is partly because there were so many longhorns -- incidental observations would occur frequently. It is also because there was more wealth in the cattle industry in Texas at the time the longhorns were still running wild. Several of the cattle pioneers in Texas, such as Charles Goodnight, had the time and inclination to observe the natural history of wild cattle. Also, J. Frank Dobie, professor at Texas A&M, interviewed ranchers, cowboys and cattle hunters of the time that shed light on the characteristics of the Texas Longhorn. Many of the observations about the behavior of Texas Longhorns apply to other wild cattle breeds.

Wild longhorn bulls were territorial. They defended a certain area and had a following of cows with calves. The average size of a family unit was 20 to 40 head. The longhorn bull would fight another bull to keep his territory. If the defending bull lost the fight, the victor would claim the territory and the cows associated with it. The longhorn bull took no part in rearing the unit's calves, except in defending the territory from predators. The whole association was relatively impersonal. Cows would sometimes move to a different territory with another bull for no apparent reason. (13)

Longhorn bulls that did not have a territory were solitary figures. Unlike wild stallions that ran in bachelor groups if they did not have a home band, the unattached longhorn bull ran alone.

Longhorn cows were relatively long-lived. They were known to produce calves annually until they were over 20 years old. Cows tended to their calves in the same manner as a doe tends a fawn. For the first 4 or 5 days, the calf would lay prone, unmoving while the cow remained some distance away. It would be nearly impossible to find a newborn calf in tall grass. The mother cow would give no indication where the calf lay. However, if a calf were threatened, it would immediately give a loud call. The entire family unit – cows and bull – would be on the spot. A nearby family unit may join them. There were no predators that could withstand the hard hooves and sharp horns of a family of angry Texas Longhorns. (14)

The following story from R.B. Townsend illustrates the care provided by longhorn cows for their calves:

"That unhappy voice told plainly enough that she was in dire distress over her calf, and I galloped up to see what was wrong. She was a big white American cow, a strain of shorthorn in her veins. There, sure enough, about three hundred yards behind her, lay her newly-born calf, under the scanty shadow of a soap-weed. She had been brought out from the States, and came of gentle domestic stock, too domestic, perhaps, for life on the range.

"The calf was not yet strong enough to follow its mother over the three long miles to the watering place, where all the rest had gone; and when his strength gave out he had lain down in the only bit of shade he could find. His mother, tortured by thirst, had hurried on without him, and then halted, with divided mind. Thirst pulled her feverishly on towards the water; mother love plucked at her heart-strings to drag her back to her calf. And here the poor fool had stood for an hour, making the prairie echo to her distracted wails, and telling any wolf lurking within a mile of her that the bell was ringing for his dinner.

"I dismounted beside the calf, picked him up, heaved him into the saddle, and climbed back and settled myself there with him in my lap.

"Small chance should I have had of doing it, if the mother had been one of my war-like Texas cows, a fierce, wild daughter of the desert. But this gentle, idiotic creature offered no objection; she was accustomed to devolving her maternal responsibilities on man, and she shambled along behind me with docile content, only lowing at intervals to tell her son she was there, as we made straight for the water-holes.

"There I left the pair, safe in the protection of numbers, a thousand head of range cattle being strung all up and down the creek.

"I turned back to the rolling prairie, and as I went I noticed half a dozen dun and brindle Texas cows, which had already slaked their thirst, traveling steadily away from the water in the same direction as myself. A few young heifers and steers accompanied them, though the mass of the cattle, as I well knew, would stay by the water till the heat of the day was over; but this party of long-horned, long-legged Texas ladies clearly had business elsewhere…. An old brindle cow with rings out to the end of her horns was leading the travelers….They struck into one of the innumerable cattle trails leading from the high pastures to the water and pressed up it, traveling one close behind the other at a steady walk that occasionally became a trot. I rode parallel to them, curious to see the goal they were making for so eagerly.

"Up we went into the high rolling sand-hills, and there, in the middle of them, in a little cup-like hollow, I saw a regular nursery. Eight little dun-colored Texas calves lay there, squatted close to the sandy ground which their coats matched so well, their heads lying out flat, with the chins pressed down on the sand, just as little antelope fawns would have crouched. In this pose they were all but

38

invisible. Beside them lay two elderly Texas cows, whose office had been to guard the calves.

"The mothers, who had travelled till now in perfect silence, began to low loudly and lovingly when they caught sight of their offspring, and in a moment each young hopeful had jumped up and rushed to his own dam, where his wriggling tail and nuzzling head, the busy lips frothing with milk, soon showed he was getting the dinner he had waited for so patiently. Meantime the two guardian cows had risen to their feet, and lost no time in starting off in their turn to make their trip to the water, leaving their own two calves safe in the care of the rest of the band. (15)

Longhorns could smell humans to the same degree as deer. Some wild longhorns were reported to prefer to die of thirst rather than approach a man-made watering hole. Longhorns could go several days between drinks of water. They were able to efficiently utilize the moisture from grasses and other plants. Dobie relates several recollections of longhorns smelling water 4, 7 and up to 10 miles away. (16) Such acute senses, wariness and sure-footed quickness made the wild longhorn a difficult game animal to hunt.

"(Longhorns) were considered to be game animals, along with deer, antelope and buffaloes. Wildlife writers in the Southwest wrote about hunting wild longhorns. As late as 1876, Colonel R.I. Dodge, whose *Plains of the Great West* remains a standard treatment of Western wildlife, wrote: *"I should be doing injustice to a cousin-german of the buffalo did I fail to mention as game the wild cattle of Texas,…animals miscalled tame, fifty times more dangerous to footmen than the fiercest buffalo."* Another military man, whose experiences were confined to the decade following the Civil War, testified, *"It is much more difficult to get a shot at a wild Texas cow than it would be at the most cautious* and wary old buck. To kill a buffalo is but child's play compared to it." (17)*

There is no athletic drama in the human world to compare with the fight of two longhorn bulls. These two antagonists were the heaviest wild animals to engage in battle in North America. Wild longhorn bulls seldom fought to the death.(18) Their size, brute strength, long horns and determination in battle made them a spectacle to behold. Among the millions of wild longhorns, fighting over territories was a common occurrence between the mature bulls and their younger challengers. Wild stallions put on fierce displays and vicious kicks, but they did not clash – head to head – like the longhorn. The paws of a grizzly are deadly, but not as sure as the horn of a maddened longhorn bull. And, the longhorn bull outweighed the average grizzly by as much as a thousand pounds.

On occasion, ranchers would capture two wild longhorns and arrange a prairie bullfight. According to one observer, words cannot capture the rage and power of the event. The bellowing and roaring, clashing and pawing. The event could go on for hours before one bull had no strength to continue and would abandon the fight. Wild longhorn bulls seldom fought to the death.

BEHAVIOR ON TRAIL DRIVES

The behavior of the longhorns on trail drives doesn't reveal much about their behavior in the wild. But some of their antics and behaviors are unexpected, so they are included here.

Longhorns normally grouped in relatively small family units. They never came together in large herds like their cousins the bison. So a herd of 1,000 to 3,000 longhorns on a cattle drive was unnatural.

In the wild, the longhorn family unit had a pecking order, much like that of other wild animals. Whether it was for a preferred grazing spot or standing in line for a drink of water, the stronger cattle had the upper hand.

During a roundup the family unit was usually broken, with some members caught while others escaped. A 2,000 or 3,000 member trail herd was made up of cattle from different family units. Still, they organized themselves in a consistent pattern.

"Handled properly, a trail herd, no matter how wild the individuals making it up might be on their native ranges, generally became, within a short period of time, a perfect traveling unit. There was always a leader, who assumed his place at the head of the herd and there kept it day after day. Behind him in a color-splotched ribbon that stretched out from a quarter of a mile to two miles or more ... the other cattle found their positions and without much variation maintained them. The stronger, more alert and energetic animals inclined to work towards the lead, the weak and lazy toward the rear. The "drags" might be sound of feet, limb and wind, and in good flesh, but from the day they started they had to be pushed ... until the end. If a forward animal became footsore, it would drop back, but after its feet healed it would take its old position...In a beef herd, most steers had 'traveling pardners', and when in any kind of mix-up these pardners became separated, they would go bawling until they found each other." (19)

On occasion lead animals were trailed back home to be employed again on another trail drive – if they were good enough. Charles Goodnight's steer "Blue" was legendary as a lead steer.

(On Blue's first trail drive)*"...from the day the herd trailed out he asserted his natural leadership. Every morning he took his place at the point and there he held it. Powerful,* sober and steady, he understood the least motion of the point men, and in guiding the herd showed himself to be worth a dozen extra hands…After leading a thousand steers all day, Blue believed in exercising the privileges of individuality. He considered himself always apart from the masses. He would walk right into camp among the pots and pans and eat pieces of bread, meat, dried apples – anything the cook would give him or the boys could steal from the cook. Often he was hobbled and left to graze with the saddle horses. Sometimes he was staked out at the end of a long rope. He preferred to bed down away from his inferiors."

"After this trip up the trail as bell ox, Blue's occupation for life was settled, but besides leading herds to Dodge City, he was put to various uses…If an outlaw steer was roped in the cedar brakes and had to be led in, he was necked to Old Blue, the pair was turned loose, and, straight as a crow flies, the bell ox would bring him to camp."

For eight years Old Blue kept at his occupation of leading herds. Some years he went up to Dodge City twice…All told, ten thousand head or more of the J A cattle followed Blue and his bell into the shipping pens of the 'Cowboy Capital'. (20)

The long cattle drives from Texas to eastern railheads or new pastures in the northern plains began about 1860. By then there were some cattle under moderate control by Texas ranchers and millions of wild longhorns to drive. Most drives consisted of a mix of moderately tame cattle and wild cattle. After about 10 days on a trail even the wildest animals conformed to the routine of being driven. (21)

It didn't take a large crew to control most cattle drives, but the crew had to be skilled at controlling cattle, sensing their mood, getting them to cross obstacles like streams or rivers and turning them back during a stampede. Cattlemen, or "cowboys", came to love working with cattle and it became a way of life that offered more than monetary rewards. Becoming skilled at the work and being among the few who did it well brought a kind of respect to the cattle drivers. And, the challenge of danger from the cattle, Indians and weather added to the sense of adventure that some men seek.

It only took a crew of about 10 cowboys and a chuck wagon cook to drive some thousand longhorns the distance of these trails. But the cowboys had to be skilled. There were many instances of cattle buyers who tried to drive a herd with rookie horsemen and lost the whole bunch. The horsemen would lose some of the cattle in an initial stampede. Then, some might escape as the drive continued the next day. Eventually, the entire herd would escape and find its way back to open range or their home ranch. (22)

One method of keeping a herd together was to include calves with their mothers in the drive. If a stampede started and the cows were separated from their calves, the cows would begin worrying more about their calves than the stampede, stop, bawl and slow down the stampede naturally. With wilder herds, however, the calves would simply be trampled to death without slowing the stampede. (23)

Calves were sometimes born on the trail. Usually, the calves were killed and left behind to keep the drive on schedule. Some drivers chose to save the calves by throwing them into a calf wagon. Charles Goodnight initially had difficulty in getting mother cows to accept their young after they were unloaded from the calf wagon in the evening. A half-dozen or twenty calves jostling together during the day would get their scents mixed, making each calf a stranger to its mother. Goodnight overcame the difficulty by putting a loose sack over each calf, so marked that it was used on the same calf day after day, being removed each evening; thus the scent proper to a calf would be retained for recognition by its mother. (24)

Aside from Indians, stampedes were the most dangerous part of the drive for the cowboy. Stampedes often occurred at night and could be set off by any number of things. Normally it would be something that startled the cattle. Being wild or mostly so, the longhorns didn't stop to think when they were startled – they just ran. A seasoned crew could turn the lead cattle in a stampede, even in the dark, so that the entire herd turned back toward the bedding ground and slowly wound down in a circular "mill" and stopped.

Lightning was often the cause of a stampede, but the cowboys would be prepared as the storm approached. A stampede could start from the howl of a coyote; the scent of a wolf; the smell from a distant chuck-wagon; a skittish steer among the herd; a gunshot; or something that only the cattle could sense. Dobie: "Some stampedes took such odd forms that almost any story about the subject is believable." (25) The unknown origin of many stampedes added to the mystique of a cowboy's life.

The wild cattle in a trail herd seemed to be perpetually on edge. Most stampedes started in an instant. Goodnight: *"Often three thousand steers have been dozing in peace – only a few restless old fellows on their feet – with the night riders circling around them at an easy gait. Then 'something happened', and with unbelievable suddenness, as quick as the flash of a wakeful eye and as unexpected as the flush of a covey of hidden quail, and with an unearthly roar that was the blending of innumerable hoofbeats, with the distinct quaking of the earth as if in fear itself, the cattle were up together and gone. A moment, a second, an instant ago they slept in peace, comfortably scattered and headed to* every point of the compass. And yet they rose, they flashed to their feet, apparently all headed in the same direction, and in impenetrable but perfectly coordinated mass, they stampeded." (26)

THE TEXAS LONGHORN VS. MODERN CATTLE BREEDS

The Texas Longhorn was not looked upon favorably by cattlemen in the Eastern and Midwestern United States, to put it mildly. Longhorns served a purpose when cattle were scarce after the Civil War and when they were so numerous as to be free for the taking. But longhorns quickly fell out of favor when modern cattle-raising techniques were adopted. Cattle were preferred that gained weight fast under modern feeding regimens.

The following represents the anti-longhorn position of many cattlemen. From 1868:

"They are tall, lank, and bony, coarse headed, with enormous horns....Their legs are long and coarse; they have much dewlap and little brisket; are flat-sided, swayed in the back, high in the flank, with narrow hips and quarters, great offal (soft tissue organs and trimmings) *in proportion to their consumable flesh....Their meat must be stringy, tough and of coarse quality. Wild and savage in appearance, they looked scarcely more civilized than a herd of Dacotah Buffaloes."*

"As an economical animal to a farmer of the Northern, Middle, or Western States, they can be of little value, as the cows give no more milk than will raise a calf till it is old enough to graze. The bullocks are too light for heavy work, although sufficiently active; and for beef, where a choice article is in demand, their value must be low. Some of the improved breeds may be crossed upon them to advantage,

no doubt, but it would take several generations to breed their coarseness and wild nature out. It is a question whether it would not be cheaper to introduce our better natives, even into their own country, with which to commence a profitable herd. The common run of Texan cattle must be doomed to extinction, ultimately, before the better breeds." (27)

In the late 1800's, ranchers saw value in crossing pure Longhorns with improved cattle from the eastern United States and Britain. Within decades the Longhorns and Longhorn mixes were replaced by improved beef breeds such as the Hereford, Angus and Shorthorn. Dairy breeds, especially the Holstein-Friesen, replaced the milk-producing Longhorns. The pure Longhorn breed almost became extinct by the 1920's. (28)

PRESERVATION OF THE LONGHORN BREED

In 1927, the United States Forest Service established a Longhorn herd in semi-wild conditions in the Wichita Mountains Wildlife Refuge in Oklahoma. In assembling the Wichita Mountain herd, experts chose only specimens that were thought to be true to type for the Texas Longhorn breed. This herd continues today. Several private ranches also kept herds of Longhorns thought to be derived from true Texas Longhorn lines.

The Texas Longhorn Breeders Association of America was established in 1964. Since then, there has been a registry of Texas Longhorns. Other Longhorn breed associations have also come into being. Longhorns are raised in many parts of the United States, often as a hobby or curiosity, but with the goal of preserving the breed.

CONTACTS AND PRESERVATION GROUPS

To locate existing herds of "certified" Texas Longhorns:

1. Wichita Mountains Wildlife Refuge (Oklahoma), U.S. Fish and Wildlife Service

2. Texas Longhorn Breeders Association of America

3. International Texas Longhorn Association

4. Various states also have breeders associations

CHAPTER THREE – WILD HORSES OF FLORIDA AND THE COLONIES

Horses came on Columbus's second voyage; wild horses were common in Florida and the Colonies; the Florida Cracker Horse came from 300 years in the wild; efforts to preserve the Florida Cracker Horse; horses often were pastured on islands on the east coast; the only remaining wild horses are on these islands; uncertainty about the origin of the island horses.

Horses are companion animals and, as such, have a bond with people that other farm animals do not. It can be intoxicating to find horses that are living free and apparently in their natural surroundings. Residents on the East Coast of the United States can visit horses that fit this description in Florida, Maryland, Virginia, North Carolina and Georgia. While they may not be direct descendents from the original horses imported into the Colonies, many of these free-ranging horses have lived with minimal human interference for generations – some perhaps as long as 300 years.

As with cattle and swine, there were no horses in the Western Hemisphere until the arrival of Europeans. Once they arrived, horses escaped and ran wild in all parts of the country. Since horses were not as adaptable to the new habitat as cattle and hogs, their wild populations were smaller. But horses have run wild in the United States at least since 1565 and continue to this day.

THE INTRODUCTION OF THE HORSE

Christopher Columbus brought the first horses to the Western Hemisphere on his second voyage in 1494. The horses were an important component of the new settlement of Isabella. They were used for transportation and working the land. But their most valuable asset was the advantage they gave the Spaniards in subduing the native populations, wherever the Spaniards went. Indians had never seen a horse and a rider. The power that the horse provided the Spanish warriors led some Indians to view the horse in a god-like fashion. Several historical references mention the horror that Indians experienced the first time they saw the rider dismount from the horse – as if the creature could break in two pieces and put itself back together again. (1)

As with cattle and swine, horses escaped to the wild and were well adapted to the New World. Wild horses could be found for decades on the islands of the West Indies after the Europeans arrived. There were not as many wild horses as cattle and pigs, however.

Indians killed wild horses to keep them from the Spanish. The Spanish settlers allowed cattle to increase because they had value for hides and meat, while wild horses often were considered a pest. And, horses did not fit into as many niches in the new environment as cattle and swine. Horses are animals of grassland. They cannot thrive in forests or marshy areas. Still, the horse, wild or ranched, flourished in the West Indies and provided seed stock for the first horses in the United States. (2)

WILD HORSES IN FLORIDA

Juan Ponce de Leon brought the first horses to Florida in 1521. It is unlikely that any of these horses survived to form the basis for wild bands. Pamfilo de Narvaez in 1527 and Hernando de Soto in 1539 also brought horses to Florida. It is unlikely that any of their horses survived.

In 1565, Pedro Menendez de Aviles established the first permanent Spanish settlements in St. Augustine, Florida, bringing horses along with other domestic animals. Within a few years horses were established in Florida. Some horses escaped and found their way into the grasslands and wild areas of Florida. A stable population of wild horses flourished in Florida. (3)

Distinct breeds of horses were brought to the United States. The Spanish imports were the Andalusian, the

Berber and the Jennet. Europeans had been selectively breeding horses for centuries before they were introduced to the United States. Europeans placed greater emphasis on improving horse breeds than any other domestic animal.

Each of these Spanish breeds was relatively small – 14 to 15 hands tall, known for their agility and endurance. Because of these features, they were ideal war horses. Their heads were straight, sometimes with at slightly convex profile. Their backs were short to medium in length. The features were fine and their stance was very balanced. (4)

The Andalusians and Berbers were mostly solid colors of gray, black or bay. Chestnut, brown, buckskin and palamino were likely imported, as well. White stockings and facial markings also occurred. The Berbers also had spotted patterns. The pinto and appaloosa colors were likely transferred from Spain to the New World via Berbers. Andalusians had longer manes and tails, a feature that was amplified in the Florida Cracker horse and the wild Spanish mustangs. (5)

In Florida, generations of these Spanish-type horses were subject to natural selection in the wild for nearly 300 years -- from 1565 to the mid-1800's. These relatively small horses became disease-resistant, sure-footed, at home on the Florida prairie and durable under the hot, humid conditions. They seemed to be naturals at herding cattle. They became a distinct breed, commonly called the Florida Cracker horse.

Florida remained very scarcely populated until 1821 when the United States claimed Florida as a territory. Several hundred thousand Cracker Horses lived in the wild without human contact for all that time. These Cracker Horses were a pure breed from the original Spanish imports. There is no record of English, French, Dutch or other breeds of horses coming down from the northern Colonies until Spain ceded Florida to the United States.

Cracker Horses remained relatively pure blooded until the early 1900's when quarter horses and other breeds were introduced. No doubt, Bone Mizell rode a Florida Cracker Horse.

PHYSICAL DESCRIPTION OF THE FLORIDA CRACKER HORSE

Florida Cracker horses are relatively small – 13.2-15.2 hands high. They range from 700 to 1000 pounds. The neck is narrow, the chest is medium to narrow and the back is short. The head is straight in profile. All of the colors of the Andalusian, Jennet and Berber breeds can be found in Cracker horses. (6)

WILD HORSES IN THE EARLY COLONIES

Horses were brought to all of the early settlements on the East Coast of the United States. Horses were the main means of transportation at the time.

The English brought their breeds of horses to New England and Virginia. The Dutch brought theirs to New Amsterdam (New York). Swedes brought horses to Pennsylvania. Some French horses found their way to the colonies via Canada. A few Spanish horses were traded from Dominica or Cuba. In general, the colonists preferred larger horses that would be more helpful in clearing and tilling the land and also capable of providing transportation. Pennsylvania became known for its large draft horses, including the Conestoga horse -- a distinct, uniform breed developed to haul goods from the Atlantic Ocean to the Ohio River. (7)

Horses were tended with the Open Range system. Resources were not available to build fences or tend the horses. They were free to roam, but attempts were made to use natural "fences" such as rivers, hills or dense forest land to keep the horses within a reasonable distance for roundups. Some horses were pastured on islands along the Atlantic shore as a sure way to keep them from escaping.

Early on, horses escaped and multiplied in the wild. Virginia was the most welcoming environment for horses, as it was for cattle and swine. Wild horses by the thousands were living in Virginia as early as 1670 when the legislature prohibited the importation of more horses.

A passage from Beverly's History of Virginia, published in 1705 shows how common it was to find wild horses in colonial Virginia:

"There is yet another kind of sport, which the young people take great delight in, and that is the hunting of wild horses; which they pursue, sometimes with dogs and sometimes without. You must know they have many horses foaled in the woods of the uplands, that never were in hand and are as shy as any savage creature. These having no mark upon them belong to him that first takes him. However, the captor commonly purchases these horses very dear, by spoiling (his best horse) in pursuit, in which case he has little to make himself amends, besides the pleasure of the chase. And very often this is all he has for it, for the wild horses are so swift that 'tis difficult to catch them; and when they are taken 'tis odds but (were past their prime), or else being old they are so sullen that they can't be tamed". (8)

As with Open Range tending of cattle, there were disputes about the ownership of horses running in the wild and attempts to limit the number of wild horses. Each colony handled this situation a little differently.

Pennsylvania required that the owner of a horse give it a double brand – one for the owner and one for his town. Double branding helped identify the owner of stray horses with more certainty. Maryland allowed anyone to shoot a wild horse that didn't appear to belong to someone. Connecticut required that all horses running loose should be castrated. In hopes of improving the size of horses generally, some colonies required that only stallions of an adequate size could run free. Smaller horses had to be castrated. (9)

The wild horses of the Colonies remained mixed breeds with new infusions of types every so often. So, they never became a distinct type like the Florida Cracker. They ran wild on the East coast from the mid-1600's until about 1800 when even the most remote parts of the East were settled.

The only remaining wild horses on the East coast are found on Assateague Island and some barrier islands of North Carolina. Cumberland Island, South Carolina has some free-roaming horses that were introduced during the 20th century.

WILD HORSES ON ASSATEAGUE ISLAND

Assateague Island is a barrier island off the Maryland and Virginia coasts. It is about 30 miles long and barely a half mile wide in most places. There is no agricultural land on the island because the soil is mostly sand. Free-roaming horses have inhabited the island for over 300 years. There is no historical record of how the original horses came to Assateague. They did not come from an abandoned farmstead because there have never been any farms on Assateague. (10)

Colonial farmers in Maryland and Virginia often used islands for pasturing horses. It is likely that farmers left some English breeds of horses as the original source of horses for Assateague.

It is popular to speculate that the original horses came from a shipwrecked Spanish galleon. If so, it could be claimed that the horses are descended from the original horses that were brought to the United States. However, there are no documents to support this theory. If the horses did come from a shipwreck, it could just as well have been an English ship, a Dutch ship or a French ship. French pirates who operated out of Dominica (see chapter 2) were known to drop off a few horses on various islands to establish herds that could be used later for food if the pirates chose to hide out on that island. Perhaps French pirates dropped off a few horses on Assateague.

During the late 1700's and early 1800's the horses of Assateague were owned by private citizens. Some brought new horses to the island and took desirable horses from the island. There is no way to know which breeds were introduced at that time. (11)

Several infusions of other breeds of horses have been made in the past century.

Shetland ponies were interbred with some of the horses in the early 1900's. Two buckskin Spanish Barb ponies were introduced to the Virginia part of the island. Since their offspring resemble horses that would have come from a Spanish shipwreck, they are favored. In 1978, 40 mustangs were brought to Assateague from BLM management areas in the Western United states. (12) Theoretically, these introductions would also carry Spanish blood, but even these Western mustangs were no longer pure Spanish Mustangs.

Whatever their origin, the horses on Assateague are no longer pure Spanish. This does not diminish the fact that some horses have existed on the island for over 300 years with very little human intervention. And they continue in a wild state today.

There is a fence dividing the Maryland and Virginia herds. Each herd is managed slightly differently. The Virginia herd is managed for a maximum of 150 horses. An annual auction is held if necessary to reduce the size of the herd. The fire department of the nearby town, Chincoteague, herds the horses across a narrow channel of water for the auction. The spectacle of the herding makes this a popular event.

The Maryland herd size is managed by administering a birth control drug at various times. The Maryland herd also has about 150 horses, but the exact number has varied more widely than the Virginia herd. Aside from the annual herding in Virginia and the birth control in Maryland, the horses are allowed to live freely. Most of them remain very wild. They form familial bands in a similar manner to all wild horses. (13)

Because they exist in a relatively small area, the behavior of the Assateague Ponies has been studied extensively. Even though there have been some introductions of domestic horses, the behavior of Assateague Ponies is similar to other wild populations – they form distinct family units (bands), with stallions competing for dominance.

Misty of Chincoteague by Marguerite Henry is a popular novel and movie about a real Assateague Pony. The success of the book adds to the attraction of the island ponies.

WILD HORSES ON THE OUTER BANKS

The Outer Banks are a string of barrier islands off the coast of North Carolina. The islands extend for about 175 miles. Some of the islands have been inhabited and livestock have been raised on some of the islands.

There have been free-roaming horses on many of the Outer Banks islands for centuries. Many of the horses were brought by the first English settlers of the islands who moved south from the Virginia tidewater area. These settlements began in about 1650. The first written record of settlement is dated 1663. English settlers brought horses, cattle, swine and other livestock to the islands.

Horses were allowed to range freely on the islands. Fences were constructed around crops to keep livestock out, if necessary. Livestock production was the only agricultural enterprise on some of the islands. (14)

As time went by, some of the livestock were abandoned. Others escaped. Free-roaming horses became almost wild on the islands. Several thousand horses were on the Outer Banks at the height of their population. There are few records about how much management of the horses occurred in the 18th and 19th centuries. It is likely that farms were started and stopped; various breeds of horses were introduced and withdrawn; and the free-roaming horses on the islands became a mixture of several breeds. There is no unbroken record of horses living in a wild state on the islands over the centuries. This is not to say that some of the bands of horses could not have remained wild the whole time. There is just no way to know.

In the 20th century, various government agencies and private groups have kept better records about the livestock on the islands. Considerable controversy surrounded the presence of horses, cattle, sheep, swine and other livestock roaming free on the islands. It was felt that the livestock were harming the natural ecosystem of the Outer Banks. Finally, in the 1950's, all livestock were removed from all of the islands except Shackleford Island. Due to public pressure, horses were allowed to remain on Shackleford Island – cattle, swine, etc. were removed. (15)

Why were horses allowed to remain on Shackleford? Largely because the inhabitants of Beaufort, North Carolina wanted to keep them. Shackleford Island has not had any permanent human inhabitants for over 100 years. A hurricane in 1933 cut off Shackleford Island from the string of other Outer Banks islands. The horses on Shackleford were perceived as living in the wild longer than horses from other islands.

There are about 120 wild horses on Shackleford Island today. It is thought that this number is sustainable. Their appearance has not changed much since the first photographs were taken more than a century ago. They are relatively short horses with long manes and tails – characteristics that are similar to other wild horses that have been subject to natural selection in a harsh environment. The 120 horses are similar in type – suggesting that there have not been any outside introductions for several decades. (16)

A popular theory about the origin of the Shackleford horses involves shipwrecks of Spanish galleons in the 1500's. If true, this would give the horses a more colorful history. Unfortunately, there is no historical documentation of this theory. And, given the potential for mixing with numerous sources of other breeds, it is very unlikely that the Shackleford horses are pure Spanish or even mostly Spanish. And, they did not run free in a wild state over all those years. Still, the theory lives in films, poems and other romanticized versions of the history of Shackleford horses.

There are three other herds of horses on the Outer Banks. There are a few horses similar to the Shacklefords in the nearby Rachel Carson Estuarine Reserve. This small nature preserve has very little habitat capable of supporting wild horses, but there is some. They have a similar history to the Shackleford's. There is a small herd (about 20 horses) on Ocracoke Island. They have been penned since 1959 to prevent them from over-grazing the island and to protect the horses from traffic on a new highway. The Ocracoke Island horses are maintained by the National Park Service. For similar reasons, the Currikuk Island horses have been restricted to a 1,800 acre fenced-in area that is owned by the U.S. Fish and Wildlife Service. Fewer than 100 horses remain in the Currikuk herd. (17)

SEMI-WILD HORSES ON CUMBERLAND ISLAND

Cumberland Island is a relatively large barrier island off the state of Georgia. It has been inhabited at various times during its history. It has a herd of about 150 horses roaming freely on the island. This herd is not as wild as the Assateague or Shackleford horses, however.

Some tourism literature for Cumberland Island makes the claim that the horses are also descended from a Spanish shipwreck in the 1500's. In Cumberland's case, this is not very likely.

Cumberland has had a long series of private owners who have brought in new horses and taken out existing horses. English settlers in the mid-1700's brought horses to the island and established farms on the island. Most of the horses were removed from the island during the Civil War to be used in the war. The Carnegies bought land on the island and introduced Tennessee Walker, Quarter Horses, Paso Fino and Arabian breeds of horses. Through the mid-1900's island residents had several breeds of horses on the island. In 1921, the Carnegies imported 31 mustangs from Arizona. (18)

The National Park Service bought Cumberland Island in 1972, but it has not implemented a management plan for the horses because of extreme differences between pro-horse and anti-horse groups. Despite the National Park Service ownership, a resident introduced 4 Arabian horses to the herd in the early 1990's.

So, they are there. Free-roaming horses of mixed origin. Despite not being as wild as other herds, they are still enjoyable to watch, especially with a background of crumbling ruins of stately mansions from a time gone by.

GO SEE THE ISLAND HORSES!

The horses on Assateague, the Outer Banks and Cumberland are a unique natural resource. They are close to the major population center of the country. They are a reminder of another time in history. They punctuate the beauty of the barrier islands. When you know their story, you appreciate them all the more. A trip to any beach can be a lot of fun. Take a trip to these beaches and you will come away with the feeling that you have *really seen something rare.*

CONTACTS AND PRESERVATION GROUPS

To located existing herds of Florida Cracker Horses:

1. The Florida Department of Agriculture and Consumer Services Division of Animal Industry

2. Florida Cracker Horse Association

To visit the Island Horses:

1. Assateague Island National Seashore (U.S. National Park Service)

2. The Foundation for Shackleford Horses

3. Cape Lookout National Seashore (U.S. National Park Service)

4. Cumberland Island National Seashore (U.S. National Park Service)

CHAPTER FOUR – MUSTANGS, WILD HORSES OF THE WEST

The appeal of the wild horse; the Spanish Mustang came through Mexico to Texas; Indian tribes helped distribute mustangs throughout the West; mixed breeds created the modern mustang; behavior in the wild; stories of mustang spirit, endurance and mystique; mustang hunting; famous mustangs; battle to save the mustang; current management by the BLM; efforts to preserve Spanish Mustangs and modern mustangs.

The horse is a beautiful animal. Graceful and commanding, viewed from a distance, there is no sight in nature like a band of wild horses running free across a western landscape. The aesthetic appeal of the wild horse is its greatest asset. Because of the imagery that the wild horse conveys, it is often considered a symbol of American power and independence, much like the bald eagle.

Horses are also valued as companion animals. There is a bond between humans and horses that is often written about in fiction, poetry and animal husbandry. This bond is transferred to the wild roaming horses. It gives the wild horse a value that is not held by other domestic animals gone wild.

Aside from aesthetic appeal, the wild Spanish Mustangs did not have a great deal of value in early America. They were not used for food. They were so plentiful that their hides had little value. As an example, if a settler to the Great Plains happened upon 1,000 wild cattle, he could set up a very profitable ranch and expand to become a Cattle Baron. If the same settler came upon 1,000 wild horses, he would have 980 more horses than he needed.

The image of the wild horse is in stark contrast to the economic value of the wild horse. Wild horses were considered pests by nearly all of the settlers of the American West. They ruined grassland by grazing the grass down to the roots – worse than sheep. They trampled ecologically sensitive areas. They muddied sparse drinking water by playfully rolling in the mud holes on the prairie. They lured valuable domestic mares away from the ranches. Wild horses were hunted and killed like varmints.

An impassioned conflict over the value of these animals has continued for more than a century.

INTRODUCTION INTO MEXICO, TEXAS AND THE PLAINS

The first horses to reach the mainland of North America were the 16 horses of Hernando Cortes. They landed in Mexico in 1519. The descriptions of these 16 horses were proudly recorded by Cortes -- a testament to the value the Conquistadors placed on their horses. These horses, along with additional shipments of horses, provided Cortes with the means to conquer Mexico and beyond.

Hernando de Soto started his ill-fated campaign with 300 horses in 1538. He traveled from Florida through much of the Southeastern United States before his search ended in Arkansas. Some historians believe that the abandoned horses of de Soto provided the seed for the hundreds of thousands, if not millions, of mustangs. Maybe so.

Francisco Coronado led an expedition including over 1,000 horses into the Southwestern United States in 1540. Numerous horses were reported to have escaped. It is possible that their descendents were among the wild horses of the American West. Again, there is no way to know.

The most likely source of the Spanish Mustang was the rapidly-expanding wild horse population of Northern Mexico in the late 1500's. Juan de Onate started a ranch in New Mexico with some of these Spanish Mustangs in 1600 – the first permanent Spanish settlement in the Southwest. His horses are known to have survived, with many escaping to the wild. Missions brought even more Spanish horses to Texas in the early 1600's. Some of these horses escaped or were run off by Indian raiders. By the mid-1600's, wild horses were ranging into the prairies of the Southwest. By 1700, wild horses were present in most of the American West. (1)

The original introductions were pure Spanish horses of the Andalusian type. The wild horses of Northern Mexico had been through 25 to 30 generations of natural selection in a harsh environment. As they ran wild in the United States for another 150 years they adapted even more to the conditions of the Western plains, becoming a distinct wild type. The Spanish Mustang became smaller. It had a longer head with longer manes and tails and an over-all "scruffy" look. Spanish Mustangs were often called ugly little horses – but it was usually said as a compliment. The Spanish-type horses were renowned for their endurance and ability to thrive on meager rations and little water. They were sure-footed from generations of running on the rocky deserts and prairies. Their hooves were hardened and they would not become foot-sore as quickly as other horses. Spanish Mustangs were used as cow ponies. The Plains Indians quickly adopted horses and spread them to all of the Western tribes. What came to be known as the "Indian pony" was a nearly pure Spanish Mustang.

American settlers preferred a larger horse. Larger horses had an advantage in military actions and were thought to be safer when herding cattle. When ranches became established in Texas in the mid-1800's, many ranchers brought along larger breeding horses such as the Kentucky thoroughbred and Quarter horse. Some Texas ranchers got improved horses from ranches in Mexico that had already mixed the Spanish horses with larger breeds. Many ranchers brought American Horses – a mix of Thoroughbred and Morgan, among others – to mix with their mustangs. The American Horse was larger and easier to handle. The mixes gave a superior horse that had endurance and handled easily. Mustangs were also mixed with draft horses, especially Percherons. A unique breed of horse from Pennsylvania called the Conestoga was used to pull the Conestoga wagons across the plains. Some of these escaped and mixed with the mustangs. By the end of the 1800's, very few pure Spanish horses remained on ranches. The wild herds on increasingly isolated ranges were also mixed breeds. Thus, the mustang has never been a registered breed of horse. The word "mustang" is used to describe several types of horses that have run free on the open range of the West. (2)

In the 20th century, more mixing of breeds occurred among the mustangs. As ranches expanded throughout the West, many breeds of horses populated the area. When cars and trucks replaced horses for transportation, whole herds of non-Spanish breeds were freed to fend for themselves. During the Great Depression of the 1930's, bankrupt farms and businesses often released their horses to the wild. The 20th Century mustang can be almost any color, any size and any conformation. The multiple colors and breeds of horses in the resulting mustang herds add to the beauty and charm of what is called a mustang today.

But it is more difficult to say that the ancestors of the present-day mustang had run free for centuries and had a birthright to the land. (3)

There is a clear distinction between the two types of mustangs. There are the pre-1850's mustangs of nearly pure Spanish blood and the 20th century mustang of mixed blood. The Spanish Mustangs were almost extinct by 1900. At present, there are some associations that strive to maintain nearly pure stock in captivity.

At the height of the wild horse population in the early 1800's, there were an estimated 2 million wild horses. (4) They were scattered through all of the states west of the Mississippi river. Wild horses were not as concentrated as the buffalo of the northern plains or the Longhorn cattle of west Texas. But they were a common sight nonetheless. For example, Lewis and Clark recorded several observations of wild horses on their expedition, but they never saw a large number in one place. (5)

HOW THE MUSTANG BEHAVES IN THE WILD

Much like the antelope, the wild horse stays in the open prairie. He relies upon speed, rather than the cover of woods to avoid capture. He is a relatively nervous creature and will run at the slightest hint of danger. The wild horse has a highly developed sense of sight, hearing and smell. A tame horse that becomes wild is the most difficult to approach. (6) It apparently has a heightened awareness of the human scent and is more wary than a wild horse that has never been fenced.

Wild horses run in bands of mares and colts dominated by a single stallion. Young stallions are forced from the band at age 1 or 2 and often roam in bachelor groups. Older stallions that lose their band to another stallion usually roam alone. (7)

One older mare normally is the second in command. She often leads the band while the stallion follows behind. Stallions were seldom caught in horse snares because the lead member of the band would be snared first. When there is a threat to the band, the stallion may cut away while the lead mare races off with the band. When either the lead mare or the stallion is hurt or killed, the band becomes disoriented and may disintegrate – moving off to some other band.

Bands of wild horses range from 2 or 3 individuals to 20 or 30. Most bands are in the 6 to 10-horse range. Large herds of wild horses, unlike the buffalo, were rarely seen. Bands will join together temporarily in the event of some perceived danger. But they do not migrate or range together. (8)

Each band is mostly territorial. The stallion will defend the territory against other stallions. If the band is chased away from the territory, it will normally return to the same territory in a few days. This territoriality obviously worked against wild horses when they were being pursued by cowboys. Experienced horse-hunters used the instinct for territoriality against the horses. If not panicked, the horses would run only within their home territory. Once tired, the wild horses were easier to capture. (9)

When food and water are plentiful, territories may overlap. The stallion will keep another band away from his harem, but will allow the other band to use part of his territory. In times of scarcity, however, each stallion defends his territory vigorously.

Bands of wild horses stay closer to watering sources than groups of wild cattle. Horses prefer to stay within 5 miles of a water source and water every day, but stay at the water hole only briefly. If the stallion senses danger at a watering hole, he may hold back while the rest of the band approaches the water. Any further alarm and the stallion vocalizes a warning. The whole band immediately runs.

The Spanish Mustang was known for the ability to go without water for days and travel great distances to a watering hole that was safe.

A band may stay together with the dominant stallion for 10 or 20 years. Because the stallion will mate with his own offspring, sometimes all the members of a single band look like the stallion. Bands with the same coloration and appearance are common. (10)

The battle of two stallions is a defining moment for the band and has been described by "Buffalo" Jones:

"They approach each other walking on their hind feet, with eyes which simulate balls of molten metal, or the electric light. Their great mouths are already open, exposing their sharp teeth, with which they inflict most terrible punishment, and in a few seconds the impending shock comes, for which each enraged animal has been preparing himself. Now their keenly cutting hoofs are flying in every direction over their adversary's body, and their powerful jaws grasp neck, shoulders, or any portion they can get hold of. They fight with all the desperation of bulldogs, throwing their whole force against each other; consequently the weaker 'goes to the wall' a terribly mutilated brute. If he is not equal in strength, or lacks endurance to withstand the awful shock of his adversary, he is at last hurled to the ground – kicked, stamped on, and torn by the teeth of his mad antagonist; and if by chance he can rise again, he rushes off, glad to escape with his life. Unlike the contests between buffalo bulls…wherein no blood is drawn, those between the wild stallions of the Plains are fraught with sanguinary results. Wherever their cruel teeth are fastened in each other's flesh,

their bodies are lacerated in the most terrible manner. When these instruments of warfare slip off the hide where they have taken hold, they snap together, sounding like the report of a firecracker...." (11)

TALES OF THE MUSTANG

The story of the early mustang is one of a marvelous, though unattractive, small horse that was renowned for its stamina, its use as an Indian pony, its fight to be free in the Wild West and its contribution to the mixed breeds of horses that helped settle the West. Stories of chasing mustangs, racing mustangs and fighting mustangs abound. Many of the stories about these mustangs have been told over and over. A sampling of the stories is included here.

Stories about the West and mustangs are often exaggerated, but there is truth in them, as well.

Mustang Spirit

"Halted in animated expectancy or running in abandoned freedom, the mustang was the most beautiful, the most spirited and the most inspiring creature ever to print foot on the grasses of America. When he stood trembling with fear before his captor, bruised from falls by the restrictive rope, made submissive by choking, clogs, cuts and starvation, he had lost what made him so beautiful and free. Only the spirited are beautiful. The antlered buck always appears nobler leaping the brush than he measures lifeless on the ground. One out of every three mustangs captured in southwest Texas was expected to die before they were tamed. The process of breaking often broke the spirits of the other two."

"Out on the plains, Josiah Gregg relates, his party 'succeeded in separating a gay looking stallion from a herd of (mustangs), upon which he immediately joined our herd and was lassoed by a Mexican. As he curvetted at the end of the rope or stopped and gazed majestically at his subjectors, his symmetrical proportions attracted the attention of all; jockeys at once valued him at five hundred dollars. It appeared that he had before been tamed, for he soon submitted to the saddle, and in a few days dwindled down to scarce a twenty-dollar hackney'." (12)

Mustang Hunting

This story is from an early 1900's farm hand and mustang hunter, Parley Paskett. Living among the mustangs for two generations, the Pasketts came to understand the behavior of the horses like few others. The depth of this understanding is revealed in this simple narrative:

"We were handling near two thousand branded range horses intermingled with about twelve hundred wild, unbranded mustangs. The horses ranged from the Great Salt Lake Desert on the east to the Idaho border on the north. They spilled over Highway 93 on the west, and to the south the border was near Whitehorse Pass along Highway 50 out of Wendover

There were 250 horses belonging to my father, Sidney Paskett, his brother George, and myself. There were also many horses, privately owned, that were not counted in this reckoning. The main body of the horses belonged to the Utah Construction Company whose horses were branded with the Wine Cup iron.

We captured mustangs any way that we could, and when we caught them we claimed them as our own if we were working for ourselves. They went to the ranching company if we were hired out. Most of the horses were small; very few were as heavy as eleven hundred pounds. The average run of them was from six hundred to one thousand pounds. The small mares were useful only as kid ponies and broodmares.

When you capture the wild mustang it takes away the illusory – almost mythical – deceptive appearance that has surrounded the wild animal. He is no longer the untouchable that has eluded man for such a time. He is now merely a captured animal to be trained for man's use. Until thoroughbreds and quarter horses came into the western picture, mustangs were the main source of saddle horses. They were tough and hardy, very useful to the cowboy.

It was early in April and we had gathered the last of nearly four hundred range horses from Squaw Creek and areas near there. The horses were grazing east of the corral. In a few minutes we would corral them, cut out the young animals to be broken to ride or work, brand the "slicks", and castrate the studs.

I heard Dad call to me and saw he was waving for me to come to him. There seemed to be no urgency, so I slowly rode to him.

"Do you remember the two yearlings we saw mating last spring – that little buckskin filly with the white front stocking and the red roan stud?" he asked as I approached. He was motioning toward a small, rough-looking animal that was suckling a skinny runt of a colt.

"Yes, I do remember", I said.

"That looks like the filly to me. What do you think?"

"I don't remember ever seeing any other animal with such a high front stocking and the buckskin color. You might be right", I said.

Dad commented, "It was a real oddity to see two yearlings mate. I've never seen that before. To see a colt mothered by a two-year-old filly is hard to believe."

The evidence was there before our eyes, and though we didn't know the actual birthday of the filly we did conclude from what we remembered that she was bred at one year old, give or take a month or two. She conceived and had a foal or colt at age two. I have never seen this happen before or since and have questioned other stockmen who have never witnessed such an occurrence.

Mustangs run in bands, bunches, herds, whatever you want to call them, of up to fifteen head. An average bunch is seven to ten and is controlled by one stud. There may be one or two yearling studs in the band, but when they become two years old the monarch, or herd stud, whips them out. These young studs then band together, two to five in a bunch, and run as bachelors until they are able to steal a mare for themselves.

It is easy to see what happens to a band of mustangs when left alone to range and reproduce naturally. One day I was riding in an area about ten to twelve miles south of Shafter, Nevada, at a place called the Ryegrass Patch. It is a hardpan area dotted with humps of half-dead greasewood and saltbrush and is flooded each spring. The day I was there, the deepest water I got into was near to my horse's knees. He was not a pony horse and I guessed the water to be between fourteen and eighteen inches deep. It covered an area of maybe forty acres, maybe eighty. I don't have any idea.

That day horses were coming in from every direction to water. Most of them had been out two or three days and were gaunt and extremely thirsty. My horse was standing well out in the water, and these bands of mustangs converged around us like a bunch of chickens after grain was thrown to them. They came as near as twenty to twenty-five yards and kept the distance from me, but never did they scare enough to run away. I rode out through the water, admiring the beautiful animals and the array of colors. Many herds of six to nine head were exact carbon copies of each other.

There were eight palominos in one bunch and I thought I'd try for one of them, but seven black horses with wide bally faces, each with four white legs, stood off to my right and I thought, maybe one of them. Behind them, however, was a bunch of eight steel-gray horses with silver manes and tails, bally faces and white legs. To one side of them were eight red sorrels with no white on them whatever. A short distance from them were six head of blood bays and a bunch of browns and several mixed bunches, as though a determined stud may have stolen a mare from each of the different bands.

The older studs had coarse jaws, heavy necks and long, tangled manes and tails, much longer manes than their counterparts raised in the mountainous country where the brush and trees combed them regularly as they ran. Younger studs were easily recognized, cagey in their actions. Some were in small groups of three to five and some had already picked up a mare or two, starting a band of their own. One particular young stud I noticed had two young mares his same color. I guessed the old monarch had whipped the young stud from the bunch but had more mares than he could control, so the younger stud took two of them with him.

We called breeding father to daughter and brother to sister or mother in-breeding, and believed it would bring out *or emphasize the poor qualities in the animal. Some horsemen, mainly thoroughbred breeders, bred father to daughter trying to strengthen the finer qualities to their horses. I expect it would work either way or maybe both ways on the same animal. This was called line-breeding.*

Some of these mustangs were small and ill-shaped animals, while others were very refined and beautiful to behold. The black ballys were larger than most of the others, as were the steel-grays. I would have been happy with one of them.

Have you ever seen more than two hundred wild mustangs all running the same direction at the same time? Have you ever wondered what you might do with them when they got to the corral? Have you ever wished you could be twenty riders on twenty good thoroughbred saddle horses so you could keep all these bands of mustangs going the right direction, so you could tuck the bunches along the edges instead of having to let them go?

In the ardor, the zeal, the passion, the ecstasy of the moment, I stood high in my stirrups and galloped those horses mile after mile, wanting so much to save a good band yet not being able to actually choose which bunch might continue in the right direction. I was able to keep nine of mixed color and not the best conformation; however, one was a 'grulla' dun mare with a palomino colt and there were two young studs, both brown, that probably would grow to be good saddle horses.

That day was one of the most fun days I can remember. I suppose that is because of the enormity of the situation, the many horses, and the several colors and herd compositions of the wild mustangs. It still thrills me to remember that day and the race I had with so many mustangs. In my mind I can see them scattered over a large area, sometimes running in separate bunches. When they did mix, the studs would squeal and bite and kick, each protecting his own. Going up the valley, most of the bands were led by older mares, but when they turned back on me the monarch studs took the lead, and each was a magnificent picture as he guided his little harem back to the wilds. The stud ran ten to fifteen yards ahead of his band and they followed generally in single file.

One band of eight sorrels led by a large, brown stud came close to me and I tried to catch them, but they were too fast and too intent on remaining free. They were look-alikes except for the stud, and I believe the former monarch was sorrel and had gotten too old to defend his harem and so was whipped away by the younger, more virile brown stud.

As I watched many horses grow up around me I noticed that about half of the two-year-old fillies conceived, giving birth to colts at age three. About four out of ten of those missed foaling the following year, but were quite regular from age five to ten. A mare that became pregnant at age three or four gave birth to a colt each following spring with few exceptions. On rare occasions a mare stayed barren until ten to twelve and then gave birth to a colt each spring until fifteen or near that age. Some few mares remained barren. A mare on good feed and in strong physical condition can bring a foal each year until quite old. If her condition is not adequate she may bring a runt or deformed colt in her latest years.

The reproduction of horses that run on the range both winter and summer without supplement, as mustangs do, depends largely on the feed available and the intensity or severity of the winters. Rough winters kill the old, the crippled and the mares with foal, especially the young two year olds and the older, weaker mares. A rough, deep-snowed winter, however, brings good grass in the spring and fattens the horses. They flourish and the mares become pregnant, bringing a bumper crop the following spring. Following these severe winters you find some yearlings come through the winter and the mother dies. This is because the yearling has suckled the mother, draining her strength. When the spring comes and the mud makes traveling heavy, the mare can't muster strength enough to change from the rough winter feed to the washy spring feed and dies after bringing the yearling through far enough so it survives.

It's a rough, cruel world, strictly survival of the fittest whether it be an ugly, ill-shaped mustang or one of refinement and beauty." (13)

Mustang Mystique

One of many mythical stories about the stallion, Blue Streak:

" A beautiful horse was no less desirable to mustangers than a beautiful woman. For nearly three years, men who knew Blue Streak gave up hearth, home and even family to chase the stallion in the mountain and valley country of southern White Pine and Eureka counties.

Most of all it was Blue Streak's color that startled the eye of the horse chasers. He was as blue-black as an eggplant, with white stockings and a prominent white blaze on his face. His conformation was magnificent. He wore his beauty in a style that excited those who viewed him in a setting as wild as he.

But Blue Streak was only seen in the winters. When heavy snows made pawing for grass difficult for him and his mares, he led his band down into the lower elevations. Mustangers around Indian Creek learned to watch for him *and then give pursuit. But Blue Streak had learned that jumping was his way out of predicaments. Invariably he selected routes that posed obstacles for his pursuers. He had taught his mares to jump, too. No chase for Blue Streak could be sustained in the type of country through which he led his pursuers.*

In the early decades of this century, when Blue Streak was about six years old and had appeared for a third winter in the valley near Indian Springs, twenty men waited to chase and encircle him before he could reach the rougher mountain slopes. But Blue Streak fooled them again. A local rancher name Rube Terrill confessed that chasing Blue Streak was getting to be "as bad as booze and poker".

(Through freakish luck, Rube Terrill finally caught Blue Streak). Rube enjoyed the notice that he attracted when he rode Blue Streak into the small mining camp called Minersville. Blue Streak was at his best prancing with pent-up energy in the excitement of the surroundings.

One man hollered out an offer of five hundred dollars for the stallion. "Seven hundred wouldn't touch him," Rube responded.

A stranger in town named Abner Temple, a Salt Lake City mining tycoon and a lover of good horses, walked up to Blue Streak and put his hand on the stallions face. "I guess a thousand dollars might take him", he suggested. Rube agreed. That afternoon a private boxcar was arranged to carry Blue Streak to Salt Lake City.

In the Mormon town, Blue Streak was a sensation every time he appeared on the streets. Abner Temple boasted that he had never felt a horse under him like Blue Streak. Within a week two attempts were made to steal the stallion. Padlocks were put on the windows and doors of the stabling area." (14)

Of the many versions of the tale of Blue Streak, this one explains the attraction of man to mustang very well. In the end, as you can imagine, the story of Blue Streak normally ends with the stallion escaping back to the freedom of the hills. In some versions, Blue Streak leaps to his death to escape the pursuing men.

Mustang Endurance

The best story about Mustang endurance is not about a mustang, but about the Spanish horse that gave rise to the mustang. The book, *Tschiffely's Ride* tells the story of Aime Tschiffely, who rode 10,000 miles from Buenos Aires, Argentina to Washington, D.C. in two and a half years, beginning in 1925.

He rode a 16 year old red and white spotted criollo horse, Mancha. His pack horse was a 15 year old buckskin criollo, Gato. Both horses ran wild in the Argentine pampas until they were enlisted for Tschiffely's ride. They were the South American equivalent of the Spanish Mustang. (15)

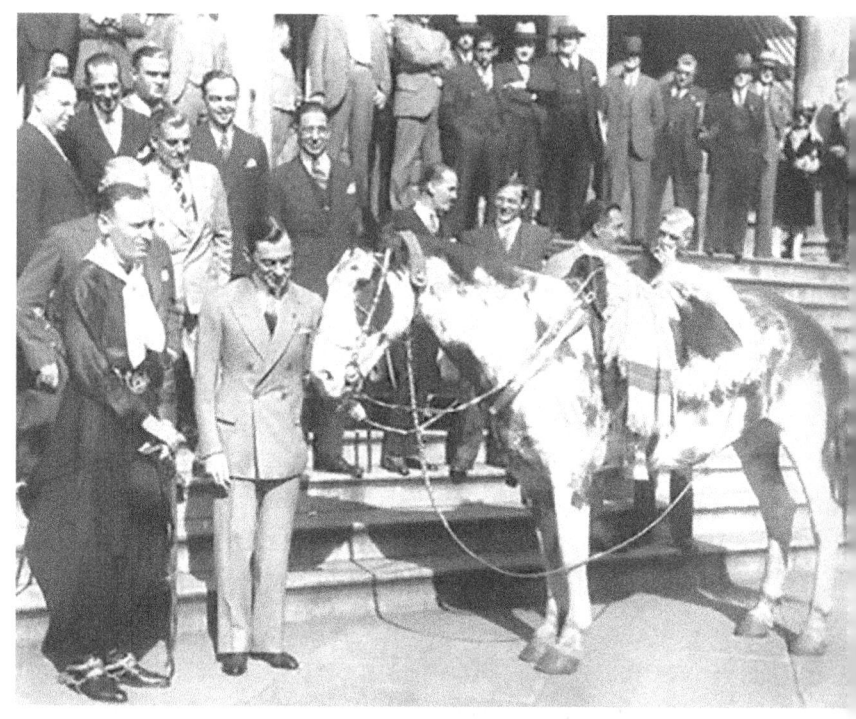

There are many other stories of the endurance of the American mustang. Some true, and some less so. Frequent tales involve an Easterner being suckered into betting on a long distance horse race between his thoroughbred and one of the small, non-pedigreed mustang, either owned by a cowboy or an Indian. After the stakes were raised, the ugly mustang would always win. Or, stories of mustang stallions that ran immense distances to avoid capture.

A recent tall tale about the endurance of mustangs made it all the way to the movies – *Hidalgo*. To the embarrassment of the movie studio, the story was a complete fabrication, according to historians who researched the claims. Still, the vast number of stories about the endurance of the American mustang suggest that endurance was one of its finest features.

WILD STALLIONS

As new towns were built on the edge of the American western frontier, settlers came into contact with wild bands of horses. Horses were the main means of transportation for everyone in the 1800's. The best horses served as status symbols to men who could afford them, much like an expensive car of today. If a bigger, faster, more perfectly formed stallion was running wild in the county, his capture lent a status beyond his monetary value.

The best mustang stallions were too fast or too durable for a single domestic horse to catch. Horse hunters often would chase a stallion in relay fashion. After scouting a stallion's territory or learning the stallion's habits from previous unsuccessful chases, the hunters positioned themselves at intervals along a chosen route. The first hunter would chase the stallion for 10 miles, for example, where a second hunter with a fresh horse would try to chase the stallion toward a third hunter, and so forth. As often as not, the wild stallion would find a rocky incline or fast-moving stream that the domestic horse would not cross and escape the relay team.

Snares were tried, but a wary stallion would let his mares march ahead and rarely be caught himself. If a trap or winged fence were placed by a water hole, the stallion would sense humans and avoid the waterhole.

Wild horse hunters would come back with tales of the stallion that got away. Somehow, the ones that got away were always the biggest and the best. Eventually, the best horse hunters in the territory took the challenge to get the wild stallion that nobody else could catch. Boys in town might dream of capturing the wild stallion. When the best horse hunters in the land were defeated by the stallion, it gained legendary status.

Perhaps the stallion was a ghost. "He couldn't be real or we would have caught him by now." And so the legend would grow. One day, a rider might come to town and claim to have shot the legendary stallion. Maybe so, thought the boys in town. But they would still see the stallion years later running free across the plains – or imagine it.

Often, the tales of the renegade stallion were very similar from place to place – suggesting that the existence of the stallion might be more fiction than fact. Almost every county from Texas to Montana had a tale about a "famous white stallion" at one time or another.

The colorful names of the famous wild stallions of the West paint a picture of the freedom they represented:

"Ghost of the Llano Estacado", "Pacing White Stallion"; "Black Dynamite", "Buckskin Joe", "Little Sagebrush", "Buckshot", "Blue Streak", "Stampede", "The Golden Stallion", "Silvertail", "Old Spook", "Red Flame", "White Fire", "Lightning", "Gunsmoke", "Gray Danger", "Glory" and "Mountain Fire".

STILL RUNNING WILD

The 20th century mustang is admired for its survival through periods of attempts to eradicate it. Even as it is quite different than the original Spanish mustang, the 20th century mustang remains a symbol of power, grace, beauty and independence. They are exciting to observe and study. They are featured in advertisements to convey a feeling of power and independence. The Ford Mustang automobile remains a popular brand that profits from these attributes.

Their detractors claim that they are not a real breed, cannot provide a gene pool for improvement of mixed breeds and continue to be a nuisance to ranches and sensitive environments.

In his book "Horse of America" published in 1897. John H. Wallace predicted the end of the American romance with wild horses:

"Fifty or a hundred years ago the pens of many writers were employed in idealizing "The Wild Horse of the Desert". He was made the leading figure in many a romance, and the hero of many a triumph. Tom Thumb, the great trotter that was taken to England, astonished all the world with his speed and his endurance, and, following the fashion of the day, he was represented to have been caught wild on the Western plains. For many years the wild horse was the "fad" of American writers, just as the Arabian was of English writers, and the writers on one side were just about as far from intelligence and truth as those on the other. When, forty years ago, great droves of the half-breeds, Mustangs, were brought from the plains to the border prairie States, seeking a market, the scales began to drop from the eyes of the worshipers of the wild horse. They were homely brutes, and they were as tough as whit-leather. But the countless multitudes that roamed at will over their grazing

grounds, making the earth tremble when they moved, have dwindled down to a few insignificant bands, and the whole glamour around the wild horse of the desert has vanished." (16)

Mr. Wallace, in 1897, was rather premature in announcing the end of the romance of Americans with the wild horse. He did not foresee the emergence of other writers, such as Zane Grey or Louis L'Amour, who further popularized the West and cowboys. Nor could he imagine the arrival of Western movies, Western television series, the animal welfare movement or the persistence of the pro-horse lobby.

Early on, the wild horses of the West had very little economic value. In fact, they were considered a pest – a wild varmint standing in the way of civilized development of the West. As early as 1824, state governments had programs to rid the prairies of what they considered to be obnoxious pests.

Relatively localized attempts were made at ridding the prairies of wild horses. Much like the grizzly bear and the mountain lion, it was acceptable for a rancher to shoot any wild horse that he saw. Some branded horses ran relatively wild, so the shooter had to be sure that he didn't kill his neighbors' horses. In the frontier, mistaken identity of farm animals sometimes led to fatal disputes. (17)

During droughts, ranchers made extra efforts to save the dwindling grassland for their cattle or sheep by hiring out the shooting of large numbers of wild horses. Horses were also driven into corrals where they were left to starve to death. In California, wild horses were herded and driven off ocean-side cliffs near Santa Barbara. (18)

By 1895 most of the good ranch land of the West was fenced off with the newly-invented barbed wire. Habitat available to wild horses became scarce. The largest populations of wild horses were limited to Nevada and the more isolated parts of other mountain states.

The population of wild horses was reduced further as the United States agreed to supply horses to foreign countries to use in warfare. Hundreds of thousands of domesticated and wild horses were sent to the Boer Wars and World War I, when Britain and other allies faced a shortage of horses. (19)

During the 1920's two new industries began to use wild horses. Horses were processed for pet food and for export to countries where horse meat was a staple of the human diet. As many as 200 pet food canneries were active in the early to mid-1900's. 8 plants processed horses for human consumption. Profit margins were low in the pet food processing business, so the capture of wild horses was done in the lowest-cost ways – sometimes accompanied by great cruelty. Mechanized mustangers, using airplanes and helicopters, sapped the last bit of romance from the old practices of rounding up wild horses in small groups by real cowboys. This industrial-scale harvesting of wild horses led to the possibility that the mustang might become extinct. (20)

The impersonal slaughter of wild horses brought about a reaction that culminated in the passage of The Wild Free-roaming Horses and Burros Act of 1971. 74 years after John Wallace predicted the end of the American romance with wild horses, they had Federal Government protection that could support a sustainable population of mustangs. 21)

But the passing of the law did not end the feud between anti-horse and pro-horse forces. They continued to disagree about how the law should be implemented. In the long run, economic values prevail. Except for tourism and the aesthetic benefit provided to the small number of people who visit the horses, wild mustangs do not have substantial value beyond the good feeling associated with the knowledge that they still exist in the wild.

The law required the Bureau of Land Management to manage the public lands where wild horses and burros existed in 1971. The BLM could not relocate the animals to other places or expand the area under management. The BLM was to provide for the welfare of the wild horses and burros while maintaining plant life in its current state.

The population size of the horses and burros needed to be controlled so that they did not degrade the habitat or become a genetically weak population. The BLM, then, has had to remove animals from the ranges every so often. The BLM sets an "appropriate management level" and works to maintain that population of animals in the area.

The total population of mustangs was estimated to be 49,658 in 1975. (22)   Currently the estimate is about 27,000.

The argument rages on about how to deal with the animals and what is an appropriate management level.

At the present time there are 3 BLM areas exclusively for horses and burros (Wild Horse Ranges) and about 200 multi-animal ranges including horses (Herd Management Areas). The Herd Management Areas are scattered across 10 western states

CONTACTS AND PRESERVATION GROUPS

To locate existing Spanish Mustangs:

1. The Spanish Mustang Registry

2. The Southwest Spanish Mustang Association

To locate existing herds of Modern Mustangs:

1. BLM's Wild Horse and Burro Program National Program Office

2. The North American Mustang Association and Registry

3. The American Mustang and Burro Association, Inc.

CHAPTER FIVE – WILD HOGS, WHAT'S FOR DINNER?

Amazing adaptability of swine to the new world; herds of pigs accompanied Spanish explorers, escaped to wild; introduced to Colonies, ran wild; became part of habitat in America; dramatic changes in appearance; behavior in the wild; millions still live in the wild; now considered a wild game animal; served as exotic meat at restaurants.

Of all the European domestic animals, swine were far and away the best adapted to life in the New World. They were brought to the mainland of North America by the Spanish, English, Dutch and French. They quickly established populations in the wild wherever they were introduced.

Wild pigs were so successful that there are currently over 2 million of them in the United States. (1) They evolved to be a major pest in many states and are hunted as game animals. The state of Missouri doesn't limit hunters to a certain season – they are such a nuisance that anyone can shoot them "on sight".

Several breeds of domestic pigs were introduced into the United States over the years. In the wild, each of them quickly reverted to the wild type - dramatically different in appearance than their domesticated cousins.

PIGS IN EARLY AMERICA

Pigs were introduced into the Western Hemisphere on Columbus's second voyage to Hispaniola – the same time as cattle, horses, sheep, donkeys and chickens. Pigs found the West Indies to be an ideal environment and their numbers exploded almost immediately. (See reference 2, chapter one)

Pigs were taken on all of the Spanish explorations and conquests of North and South America. Pork was a favored meal of the Conquistadors. Swine actually multiplied on most expeditions. For example, Hernando de Soto began his quest with thirteen sows and two boars. After three and a half years of very difficult travel, wars with Indians, disease and cold winters, his quest ended with 700 swine remaining. (2) This, after many pigs had been eaten when other provisions were short. Many pigs escaped or were driven off during battles with Indians during the de Soto expedition. It is thought that they formed the seed stock for wild pigs that still roam the Southeastern United States today.

If the wild pigs in the Southeast did not arise directly from the de Soto expedition, they escaped to the wild soon after. All Spanish settlements brought pigs as a source of food while the settlement was becoming self-sustaining. Escapees from these settlements quickly became a wild population of pigs in the Southeast.

Soon, French settlers brought pigs to Louisiana and English settlers brought pigs to the east coast of the United States. By 1650, there were wild pigs from New Orleans to Boston. Present-day wild pigs represent several hundred generations in the wild and come from many different breeds. But they all look alike – the wild type. (3)

THE APPEARANCE OF PIGS CHANGED DRAMATICALLY IN THE WILD

Domestic pig breeds look very different than their wild types. It only takes a few generations for pigs in the wild to resemble the wild type. They quickly become narrow-bodied, longer legged and higher backed. They develop short, sharp tusks. Their heads become longer, straighter and narrower. Colors soon fade to a dull brown or black. And their curly tail straightens. Only domestic pigs have curly tails. Wild pigs have straight tails. The dramatic change in appearance is a result of natural selection in action. All of the original imported pigs were domestic types. They became the wild type through adaptation to life in the wild. (4)

The color of new-born piglets changes dramatically after a few generations in the wild. Domestic piglets are normally miniature versions of their parents – solid pink, black with a white stripe, etc. The new-born piglets of wild pigs have brown and cream lengthwise stripes – an adaptation for camouflage.

While there have been no scientific studies on the amount of time it takes a domestic pig to completely revert to the wild type, notes from the Colonies suggest that wild pigs were similar to the wild type by 1650. (5) This would be 40 years after their introduction, amounting to 15 generations.

INTRODUCTION OF EUROPEAN WILD BOARS

From 1521 to the late 1800's the only swine introduced to the United States were domestic farm animals from various European countries. Europe also has a wild version of this species. Called the European Wild Boar, it has never been domesticated. It is found in most European countries and is hunted as a game animal. It is larger and more aggressive than the wild boars that arose from natural selection in the wilds of the United States. Since 1880, there have been several introductions of European wild boars into the United States for sport hunting purposes. Some were introduced into fenced hunting preserves. Others were simply let go to mix with the wild pig population. Either way, substantial numbers of them eventually escaped.

Wild Boars of New Hampshire

The first introduction of European wild boars came to New Hampshire in the late 1800's. Austin Corbin, millionaire New Yorker, established a completely fenced-in game preserve on about 25,000 acres near Cornish, New Hampshire – a present-day artist colony. He introduced wild boars, buffalo, elk and other game animals. The game preserve became known as Corbin Park. It has been managed by the Blue Mountain Forest Association since 1890. It remains an exclusive private club with wild boars as one of its game animals.

In the 120 year history of Corbin Park, there have been many escapes. There is no such thing as a secure game preserve. Early on, some locals were opposed to the big city people buying up all the land for the preserve. As a protest, they cut the fence to allow some of the wildlife to escape. Later, strong winds blew down several trees that crushed the fence, allowing more escapes. After a few decades of use, the swing gates over a creek were broken by spring floods creating another escape route. Over the years, vandals have cut numerous holes in the fence.

The wild boars that escaped from Corbin Park have never flourished in New Hampshire. There have never been over a few hundred escaped pigs in New Hampshire and Vermont. Because they cause damage to crops, they have been aggressively hunted by farmers. Inside the park, there have often been over 500 European wild boars at one time. Surplus boars have sometimes been shipped to other parts of the United States and released. (6)

Wild Boars of the Smokey Mountains

In 1908 an entrepreneur named George Gordon Moore bought 1600 acres of forested land around Hooper Bald peak in West Virginia. He built a 10-foot split-rail fence around the entire property. He built a hunting lodge and a road to get to it. In 1912 he brought in a shipment of Polish wild boars and planned to organize hunts at his luxury preserve. The wild boars proved to be more aggressive than anticipated. Only one hunt was held – several dogs and one hunter were killed by the wild boars during this inaugural hunt. The wooden fence was totally inadequate to hold the boars. Being much larger than the native wild pigs and having much longer tusks, the wild boars quickly terrorized the locals. With time, however, the wild boars mixed with the native wild pigs to form a sub-set of the wild pig population in the area. In 1923 Mr. Moore trapped some of the hybrids and released them in the Carmel Valley of California. In 1931 he released some in east Texas. There may have been other releases that remain unrecorded. (7)

HOW THEY BEHAVE IN THE WILD

Different animals have different names for a grouping – a flock, a herd, a band or a family. A group of wild pigs has a specialized term – a "sounder". It doesn't have any special meaning or reference. It is just what a family of wild pigs is called.

The typical sounder of wild pigs consists of several females and their litters. Since pigs have a relatively large number of offspring, the sounder can have dozens of individuals with only a few adult females. One adult female is usually dominant. Adult males are loosely associated with the females and their offspring. The sounder does not defend a certain territory, but they remain in the same location as long as food is available and there are no external threats to the group. The male's role as a defender of the territory is not as critical with pigs as it is with other animals. Apparently the adult females can handle any threats to the group. One territory may overlap another without friction. Several sounders may share a common watering hole or even a feeding range. If a resource becomes limited in the territory, the pigs move to a better territory. Wild pigs get along very well with other wild pigs. They don't get along with anyone else, however. They will attack human intruders, rather than flee.

Males do compete for the attention of a receptive female, but the battles are normally short and seldom fatal. Males do not compete for the ownership of a sounder. Rather, they come and go in a loose pattern. Young males form bachelor groups. Older males are mostly solitary when not staying near a sounder.

Pigs are omnivorous – they eat just about anything. They can adjust their diet from season to season depending on what is available. They seldom need to migrate from their chosen location to find acceptable forage. If they do need to move, they can usually find a new home with food that they enjoy. Wild pigs prefer woodlands but they can thrive in marshland and agricultural land. Their ability to utilize many different kinds of food gives them a distinct advantage for survival.

In addition to an adequate supply of food and water, the location chosen by the sounder must have plant material to build a "nest" and a place to wallow in mud. Wallowing plasters the skin with mud. This protects against flies and helps to regulate the pig's body temperature. The nest is the secure place where the pigs spend much of the day at rest. Foraging and eating take up the rest of the day. Pigs can be completely nocturnal, especially if they are being actively hunted. Or, they can adapt to outside influences to forage at any time of the day. They sleep in a clump during very cold weather. This attribute greatly increases the northern range of the species.

They eat, they sleep, they roll in the mud, they drive off any intruders. That pretty much describes their life-style. (8)

RARE LARGE SPECIMENS, WILD HOG ATTACKS

Wild pigs are smaller than their domestic counterparts, largely due to the rigors of life in the wild and the lack of a constant supply of food. A reduction in size is common to most farm animals gone wild. The adult wild pig males weigh around 150 pounds, the adult females slightly less. A race of European Wild Boar from Russia was slightly larger than the introductions from other sources. But they seldom weigh over 200 pounds. Rarely, specimens have been found that weigh around 600 pounds. (9)

If cornered, the male or female will attack a human. With up to 5 inch tusks and an aggressive personality, wild pigs can be dangerous. Numerous attacks are reported every year in the United States and other countries.

The aggressive nature of wild pigs gives rise to exaggerated stories about their size. Common folktales warn about wild pigs that weigh 1,000 pounds to 2,000 pounds. Such animals do not exist. An encounter in the woods with a normal sized wild boar is dangerous enough. (10)

MAINTAINING WILD PIG POPULATIONS FOR SPORT HUNTING

Wild pigs have become entrenched in the fauna of many states, despite not being a native species. It would be very expensive, if not impossible to eradicate the wild pig population. Wild pigs do considerable damage to native plants and sensitive habitats. Many states have to balance the concerns of environmental groups versus sport hunters in managing the wild pig population. Departments of Fish and Wildlife set bag limits for hunters. Studies have been done to measure the damage to sensitive environments from wild pigs. In some cases, wild pigs have been removed from sensitive areas.

The policy of most states is to maintain a viable population of wild pigs for sport hunters and use the money from hunting permits to study the environmental impact of the pigs.

WILD HOG FOR DINNER

Hunters generally eat the wild pigs that they kill, much like any other game animal. Wild pigs are the same species as domestic swine so the cuts of meat are similar. A wild pig yields almost no bacon because it is too lean. Taste is a very subjective thing. Some people prefer the taste of wild pigs over domestic pork and vice versa.

Several hundred thousand wild pigs are killed each year in the United States. There are an endless variety of recipes for preparing them. Most recommendations are for young pigs – one or two years old. The older and larger animals may develop a strong gamy flavor.

Wild pigs are often grilled whole over an open pit. Recipes abound for chops, roasts, legs, ribs, sausages and stews

Wild hog can be found in restaurants in most major cities in the United States. Typically, a restaurant that specializes in exotic meats will serve wild pig along with buffalo, elk, ostrich, rattlesnake, etc.

Wild boar has been a staple of cooking in Tuscany for centuries. In the United States, restaurants serving wild boar are easily found in Florida, Texas, California and Hawaii –states with the largest populations of wild boar. (11)

COLLEGE MASCOT

The wild boar is the college mascot at the University of Arkansas. Wild boars have been called "razorbacks" in Arkansas as long as anyone can remember. The nickname refers to the narrow humped back of the wild boar. The Arkansas football coach in 1909, Hugo Bezdek, wanted his team to fight like a wild band of razorback hogs, thus the name.

Beginning in the 1960's, the University had a live razorback as its mascot. As could be predicted, one of them escaped and behaved badly. Named Big Red III, the hog escaped in 1977 and caused some damage to crops before an irate farmer shot him. Another wild hog was said to have killed a coyote, a domestic pig and numerous rattlesnakes before it became the school's mascot. (12)

CONTACTS AND HUNTING GROUPS

1. The Wild Boar Conservation Association

2. Search online by state: Wild Boar Hunts

CHAPTER SIX – DOGS AND CATS. INVASION OF THE CARNIVORES

Indian dogs and wolves; dogs of the Conquest; Spanish dogs cannot compete with indigenous predators; dogs unable to establish long-term niche in the wild; Spanish and English dogs replace Indian dogs; dogs escape in New England and run in packs; irony of family pets becoming killers of livestock and humans; packs of dogs, like wolves, attack livestock and humans every year; current population of wild dogs and problems associated with them.

House cats came with earliest settlers; soon established as strays and scavengers; hunting instinct in house cats virtually the same as wild ancestors; only able to survive near humans and human structures; irony of family pets becoming destructive of wildlife; current population of wild house cats and problems associated with them.

Notable differences in the degree of domestication between dogs and cats.

INTRODUCTION

There were no house cats or related wild cats in the United States until they were brought by Europeans. The native Indians had semi-domesticated dogs, but they were rapidly replaced by European dogs that had been bred for size, strength or other characteristics.

The only carnivorous domestic animals introduced to the United States were the dog and the cat. All of the other domestic animals were herbivores, except the pig. Pigs were mostly herbivores but would also root for insects and small animals.

Carnivorous stray dogs quickly became a problem, attacking livestock brought by the settlers. Under harsh conditions, packs of escaped dogs were known to attack and kill humans. In early America, stray cats proved to be beneficial as scavengers and rodent-control measures. It was not until much later that the impact of stray cats on birds and other small animals became an issue. There continue to be millions of stray cats and dogs in the United States today. (1)

Neither the dog or cat established a permanent, long-term population in the wild of the United States. Thus, there has been no natural selection for a certain type of dog or cat in the wild. At the most, an escaped dog or cat might remain in the wild for a few generations before hunger, disease, predators or humans would eliminate those individuals, only to be replaced someday by other escaped or abandoned dogs and cats. The make-up of the population of dogs and cats constantly changes based on the popularity of type of dog or cat in the pet population of humans.

DOMESTIC DOGS

INDIAN DOGS

Dogs are considered to be a separate species from their ancestors, the wolves. Thousands of years ago, dogs diverged from wolves by lessening their fear of humans, thus living in a loose association with humans. Dogs also lost some of the social instincts of wolves.

Dogs migrated to North America along with humans around 12,000 years ago. Since then, the archeological evidence shows that dogs followed humans to all parts of North and South America. As Indian groups became isolated from one another, different cultures developed among Indians of the Americas. Indian dogs were modified by the environments that they inhabited and by the cultures of their associated tribes. As a result, there were several types of Indian dogs, ranging from Eskimo dogs, Plains Indian, Sioux, Mexican hairless, and Peruvian pug-nose, among others. (Allen, 1920, p. 30 of Schwartz) Many of these dogs of Central and South America were developed by purposeful selective breeding.   A small dog of the Caribbean was bred to be fattened as a food item.

There is less evidence of selective breeding of dogs in what was to become the United States. "Numerous accounts from early visitors to North America state that most native groups had dogs that resembled coyotes or wolves. Those dogs were ill-mannered, often hungry, and treated casually or harshly, and had more of a howl than a bark." (2) These Indian dogs were often camp followers, living on scraps from the tribe and used opportunistically as hunters, haulers or emergency sources of food.

It is likely that some of the Indian dogs interbred with gray wolves on occasion. Dogs and wolves are capable of interbreeding, but they do not do so in the wild, except under unusual conditions, such as the lack of a mate of its own kind.

Most Indian dogs were considered "semi-domesticated" because they seldom lived in the same structures as their masters, they were not selectively bred for specific purposes and they were not highly trained. Rather, the least wild of the bunch were conscripted for jobs and held to the task with whips, only to be let loose when the job was finished. (3)

Most Indian dogs, while not entirely tame, were also not entirely wild. They could not compete in the wild with wolves and other predators. Dogs were smaller than gray wolves and had lost the social structure that allowed wolves to survive among larger predators. Thus, Indian dogs never established a permanent wild population in the United States and always depended on humans for their niche.

Modern research has found more evidence of selective breeding of dogs among smaller tribes of Indians of the United States, most notably in Oregon and California. These dogs were kept as pets. In the Great Plains, Northeast and Southeast there is little evidence of selective breeding of dogs by the Native peoples. Rather, the dogs accompanied the Indians, as they had for millennia and any changes in appearance or behavior can be attributed to natural selection.

Great Plains Indian dogs were most similar to wolves in coloration and size. These dogs were very commonly seen with the Indians, as they were highly valued for hauling materials from site to site among these nomadic tribes. Dogs of the Northeastern states were less common, though some were trained for hunting. Often, the Northeastern dogs were solid black or black and white. In addition to wolf-like dogs, most areas of the United States also had a smaller type of dog associated with the Native Indians. This smaller dog may have been used to hunt burrowing animals and sometimes was eaten by the Indians. (4)

None of the native dogs barked. Instead, they howled or whined – as if they preserved a partial vocabulary of the wild wolves of North America. European dogs barked, suggesting selective breeding for this trait or some genetic influence from wolves of Africa which barked naturally.

From G.M. Allen's *Dogs of the American Aborigines,* 1920, pp. 449-468, these are notes about the most common Indian dogs and the ones which had the largest populations in the wild of the United States. The Plains-Indian Dog, The Sioux Dog, the Larger or Common Indian dog and the Short-legged Indian Dog (names ascribed by Allen):

The Plains-Indian Dog. "Size, medium; slightly smaller than the Eskimo Dog; ears, large, erect; tail drooping or slightly upcurved; coat rather rough, usually 'ochreous tawny' or 'whitish tawny' or sometimes black and gray, mixed with white.

Distribution: Western North America from British Columbia south perhaps to the Mexican boundary and eastward through the Great Plains Region.

Wortman....found among the Umatillas, Bannocks, Shoshones, Crows, Arrapahoes, and Sioux mongrel dogs 'which to one familiar with the color, physiognomy, and habits of the coyote, have every appearance of blood relationship, if they are not in many cases this animal itself in a state of semi-domestication'.

Teit....They were good hunters, though poor watch-dogs, and the best ones for deer hunting were highly prized. Such dogs generally ran the deer to water, often bringing it to bay in some creek, and keeping it there till the Indian came up and dispatched it.

Perhaps the earliest mention of the use of these dogs as pack-animals is found in Coronado's account of his journey in 1540 to 1542, from the City of Mexico to the Texas plains. When some ten days' march from the present Rio Pecos, Texas, Coronado and his followers came to Haxa, where the natives were found to have 'packs of dogs'. In moving camp, these Indians started off 'with a lot of dogs which dragged their possession.' They travel like Arabs, with their tents and troops of dogs loaded with poles and having Moorish pack saddles with girths. A letter from one of Coronado's men further describes the dogs. 'These people,' he writes, 'have dogs like those in Spain, except that they are somewhat larger, and they load these dogs like beasts of burden, and make saddles for them like our pack saddles, and they fasten them with their leather thongs, and these make their backs sore on the withers like pack animals....when they move, for these Indians are not settled in one place, since they travel wherever the Buffalo move, to support themselves, these dogs carry their houses, and they have the sticks of their houses dragging along tied on to the pack saddles, besides the load which they carry on top, and the load may be according to the dog, from 35 to 50 pounds.' As pack-animals, for moving camp in their pursuit of the Bison, these dogs were of great service to the Indians of the plains country, and every village was provided with troops of them."

Sioux Dog. "A large wolf-like dog, probably closely related to the Plains-Indian Dog but larger and gray rather than tawny in color."

"Distribution: Probably the north-central plains area, from the Missouri river north perhaps to Saskatchewan."

The Sioux Dog was used as a pack animal, much like the Plains-Indian Dog.

Larger or Common Indian Dog. "This was probably closely related to the Plains-Indian Dog, but seems to have been usually solid black or black and white in patches instead of resembling the coyote in color. The skull has, when adult, a knife-like sagittal crest, a high forehead, and is rather slender. Limbs much longer than the Short-legged Indian Dog yet slightly inferior to those of a Greyhound."

"Distribution: Dogs of this general type, agreeing fairly well in size and proportions were found among the forest Indians from Alaska southward to Florida and the Greater Antilles, and westward to the edge of the plains in the east central States." (Note: Very early reports and records show this type of dog to be found in Maine, Pennsylvania, Delaware, Connecticut, Rhode Island, North and South Carolina and Florida.)

Since the Eastern Indians were not as nomadic as the Plains Indians, there were fewer dogs kept in each village. The Larger or Common Indian Dog was used for hunting and, to a much lesser degree, for war and community protection.

Short-legged Indian Dog. "Ears erect, head large in proportion, the legs relatively short but not distorted as in our Turnspits. Fur of the body short and sleek, that of the tail longer. This is possibly a derivative of the Common or Larger Indian Dog."

"Distribution: It is hardly possible to trace the former distribution of this type of dog. It was found by Richardson in southern British Columbia, and a dog apparently similar is known from Quebec and perhaps formerly in New England and New York. Probably it was found among canoe-using or forest-living tribes in the North, hence was infrequent or absent in plains country."

"These smaller dogs were apparently the familiar household pets or hunting companions of the Indians of forested country or of the canoe-using tribes. They were too small to be of service as pack-animals with travois and hence seem not to have been much in favor with the Plains Indians, whose main subsistence was the Bison for hunting of which, dogs were unnecessary. Suckley (1860) particularly mentions that they were kept more as a 'playmate for the children and a pet for the women' among the tribes of the Columbia River. Moreover, a small dog is a better companion in a canoe than a larger clumsy animal."

Such small dogs were often mentioned as hunting beavers with the forest-living tribes.

Dogs that escaped from Indian encampments did not cause problems for the Indians, but found plenty of problems for themselves among the natural predators. None of the Native Indian tribes of the United States kept domestic farm animals. Wild dog attacks on domestic animals only became a problem after Europeans brought sheep, hogs, cattle and other farm animals to the United States. So, until the Europeans arrived, stray and wild dogs were just part of the normal fauna, used opportunistically, and there was no attempt to contain them or eliminate them. Things were about to change.

DOGS OF THE CONQUEST

The first dogs that may have gone wild in the United States, other than the Indian Dogs, were the war-like dogs brought by the first Spanish explorers. Columbus brought 20 dogs on his second voyage in 1494, some mastiffs and some greyhounds. These dogs were used to help subjugate the native population of Hispaniola. Each successive Spanish ship to Hispaniola brought more dogs. As with cattle and hogs, some of the Spanish dogs escaped and found a niche on the island. By 1509, the wild dogs had become a threat to game animals and livestock (5). A decree was issued to kill all of the wild dogs or capture and re-train them. It is likely that packs of wild dogs survived on Hispaniola until the island was completely settled.

The Indians of Hispaniola had only one type of dog at the time of Columbus' arrival – a small dog that was fattened for food, considered a delicacy. Eventually, the larger, more aggressive Spanish dogs were able to eliminate the native dog from the island. And so it was destined to go, as the Europeans moved on to the mainland of the United States. They brought larger, more aggressive dogs that eventually replaced every Indian Dog. Often, the Indians purposely used the imported dogs because they were larger and easier to train. By the late 1800's there were no more Indian Dogs. (6)

The dogs of the Conquest were bred and trained as warriors. In the 1400's, all advanced countries used dogs for war in some way. Dogs had been domesticated and bred as warriors for several thousand years by the Egyptians, Romans, Greeks, Mongols and many others. Prior to the introduction of accurate rifles, dogs were very effective infantrymen. Partially covered with armor or a protective coat of mail, a dog was seldom injured by arrows, darts or spears before it could wound or kill one or more enemy soldiers. These dogs were bred to have powerful jaws that tore at the flesh of its unfortunate victim. The sight of a band of dogs with the Spanish invaders was intimidating. To add to the effectiveness of the dogs as warriors and to further subjugate the native populations, the Spanish used dogs as means of torture.

The imported Spanish dogs, mastiffs, greyhounds and large hounds were larger and more aggressive than native Indian dogs. Mastiffs could weigh as much as 200 pounds and out-fight any man. The Spanish greyhounds were larger than today's greyhound breeds. They could out-run a man and were also trained to fight without mercy. Wolfhounds, bloodhounds and other hounds could also weigh over 100 pounds. As a comparison, a large gray wolf would weigh about 100 pounds and a good-sized coyote would be just under 50 pounds. (7)

As Spanish dogs escaped, it might be expected that these aggressive, large dogs could establish a permanent population in the wild of the New World. However, the lack of socialization that came with domestication seems to have stopped the new dogs from finding a permanent niche in the wild. Packs of wolves, working together, were able to drive the newcomers from their territory. And the dogs were apparently not organized enough to consistently bring down large prey, such as deer, moose, buffalo and even wild hogs. Instead, wild dogs have settled for living in the shadow of humans. As wolves and other large predators were eliminated from the frontier by humans, wild dogs were able to sustain themselves as temporary inhabitants of that space -- only to be eliminated by humans if they became too much trouble.

TYPES OF DOGS IMPORTED TO UNITED STATES

Europeans, Arabs and Asians had been selectively breeding dogs for centuries. By the time Europeans arrived in the United States, many specific breeds of dogs had been recognized. There were terriers for hunting small game, spaniels for hunting birds or waterfowl, wolfhounds for battling wolves, mastiffs and other large breeds for work or war, herding dogs and bulldogs.

All of these breeds were eventually brought to the colonies, starting with a spaniel and an English mastiff on the Mayflower. (8) As the colonies were settled, nearly every dog breed from Europe found its way to the United States. Dogs that could help with clearing land, farming and protecting isolated homes were most common – working breeds, bulldogs and collies. Various hounds for hunting, including the foxhound, soon became popular in Virginia.

Despite this wide variety of sources for wild dogs, wild dogs in the United States, much like all around the world, quickly become mixed breeds that tend toward a type. Camp followers, scavengers, street dogs – whatever name you choose – tend to be medium sized dogs, average in almost every way (length of muzzle, size of ears, height, weight, color). They are thin, never carrying extra weight. Nimble. Quick-footed. Just like other domesticated animals that had to make it on their own.

WILD DOGS IN EARLY AMERICA

Within a few decades of settlement, wild dogs became a nuisance in the Colonies. As early as 1635, Salem (Massachusetts) townsmen passed a local ordinance prescribing punishment for dogs that attacked poultry. In 1648, Massachusett's general assembly enacted a measure … to prescribe hanging as the penalty for dogs that harassed sheep. (9) A 1692 law gave Bostonians free rein to kill any dog they saw "seizing upon cowes and cattle." They did not have to inform the dog's owner, and if the owner complained, "the selectmen will beare them out in there so acting."

A similar experience with wild dogs plagued Virginia. By 1656, coordinated efforts were made to control wolves and wild dogs, due to their predation on livestock. (10)

TEMPORARY NATURE OF WILD DOG POPULATIONS, NO NATURAL SELECTION

Why didn't dogs succeed in establishing a wild population in the United States, like cattle, horses and pigs? Perhaps dogs had become too domesticated.

Cattle and horses were successful in areas that had vast amounts of their natural food – prairie grasses. But each of these species had to compete with buffalo, elk and other herbivores for resources. As we have seen, cattle and horses quickly reverted to their wild behaviors – forming tight-knit bands or families, establishing hierarchies within the family and claiming a specific territory to defend. As families, cattle and horses were able to chase off competitors and fend off predators from their territories.

Pigs didn't have it quite so easy. While cattle and horses were presented with millions of acres of grassland with few competitors and the assistance of humans in defeating competitors such as the Bison, pigs walked away from their pens into Eastern forests filled with wolves, coyotes, panthers, bears, raccoons and many other animals that competed for the same food and space or were direct predators of pigs. Again, the success of the wild hogs must have depended in great part on their ability to take up the ways of their wild ancestors. They quickly formed family units, just like wild hogs that had never been domesticated. They settled into a niche mostly held by coyotes. Being small, quick, aggressive and adaptable in location and adaptable to human intrusions, wild hogs were successful in that niche from the day the first European pigs escaped to the present day.

So, why not wild dogs? Why didn't they replace similar animals, such as wolves or coyotes?

It could be that wild dogs never had a chance to enter a truly wild part of the country. That is, humans settled the same areas as dogs; escaped dogs were a threat to livestock and humans kept the wild dog population in check. However, pigs went wild in the same places as dogs and they quickly expanded their range. Were pigs less domesticated and able to escape from the influence of humans? Were dogs so tied to humans that they couldn't even make the effort to expand into areas without humans where they could have a chance to replace wolves or coyotes in the wild?

These are questions that probably cannot be answered with certainty. There were many variables at work and there is no way to repeat the circumstances found in Early America and study the question.

Part of the answer may be found in the many ways that dogs differ from wolves and coyotes in their ability to organize packs and form a cohesive social unit. From

Sheldon, 1992, Section on Gray Wolves, pp. 39-45: "Wolves are almost entirely carnivorous and prey primarily on large mammals. A group of wolves is capable of killing a full-grown black bear. Wolves are able to prey on animals much larger than themselves only because they hunt as a cooperating pack....Wolves have the most highly developed social organization of all the Canidae, with the exception of African and Indian wild dogs. The essential social unit is the pack, typically composed of a mated pair, their offspring of the year and a few offspring from previous seasons. (Editors note: Stray dogs would take several generations to begin to form a similar pack)...Wolf packs are characterized by elaborate social interactions. Each pack inhabits and defends an exclusive home range (Editors note: much like wild mustangs)...There is little overlap between the home ranges of neighboring packs, and buffer zones exist between them. Scent marking and howling function to maintain territories. When direct encounters between packs do occur they are marked by chases and fighting, sometimes violent enough to result in death."

Stray dogs have not been observed to establish territories. They may run in groups but do not last long enough in the wild to establish wolf-like packs with a social structure.

Dogs have lost many of the socialization attributes of wolves and coyotes. This may lead to dog's inability to replace either of their two cousins in the wild, despite some dogs being larger and perhaps more aggressive than wolves and other dogs having size and specialty breeding that might make them seem more fit than coyotes for that niche.

Dogs have been domesticated a similar amount of time as cattle, horses and pigs. However, the degree of domestication has been greater for dogs. Beyond being tame enough to keep as farm animals, content to live in pens and do simple tasks on the farm, dogs have lived in closer contact with humans and have learned complicated tasks and tricks. As a result, many of the dogs' ancestral instincts, behaviors and even morphology have changed.

CHANGES IN DOMESTIC DOGS' COMMUNICATION VS. WOLVES

Most dogs bark a lot. They have been used for millennia as protectors and barking has been selected for. Wolves and coyotes, on the other hand, never bark. Instead, they have a wide variety of vocalizations – howls, whines, whimpers – that serve as communication among the pack. Dogs have lost many of these vocalizations and picked up a distinct disadvantage for living in the wild – a propensity to bark that gives away their location to predators. Wolves howl in unison. If dogs howl, they howl alternately.

Wolves and coyotes have a tail gland that secretes a strong odor, likely used for identification and hierarchy in the pack. Dogs no longer have this gland. There are remnants of the gland in some dog breeds. In particular, malamutes, German shepherd and Rhoedesian ridgebacks have coarse hair or a distinctive color to mark where the gland would have been. (11).

Wolves and coyotes have light or white colored hair around their lips which extends to their cheeks, as if outlining their mouth. It is thought that this white background accentuates facial expression and contributes to communication. Dogs often have long hair or different color hair in place of this outline, which probably detracts from their ability to communicate with each other. (12)

Wolves and coyotes have a wide variety of facial expressions. While dogs have maintained many of them, many more have been lost. Again, a possible detriment to communication among dogs.

The position of the ears of wolves and coyotes communicate fear, stress, aggression, etc. The ears of wolves and coyotes are simple, pointed and upright, able to be held forward or back, depending on the situation. Many dog breeds have ears that are much larger and hang down. Dog ears are much more difficult to be modified in position to communicate something to other dogs. (13)

OTHER CHANGES IN DOMESTIC DOGS VS. WOLVES

Wolves and coyotes have thicker and contrasting-color hair on the shoulders. This is a clear location for puppies to grab as they play-act fighting and attacking. Wolves, in particular, are extremely accurate in their strikes when attacking. They train from puppies onward to attack with accuracy, using the shoulder hairs as a target. Dogs have lost this contrast of colors on their shoulder hair and much of dogs' play-fighting is less precise than wolves. A little thing like that could become a deal-breaker in the tightly-contested world of survival in nature. (14)

Wolves defend large territories because their prey is relatively scarce. Northern wolves that prey on moose have very large territories because moose can only live in boggy areas that are usually far apart. Wolf packs must learn to make coordinated attacks on large mammals to bring them down. Young wolves learn to join in these attacks by "observational learning and experience of trial and error"…"this latter pattern of rushing directly forwards and slamming (another young wolf) with the shoulder or hips was seen early in life only in the wolf during play fighting". (15) Domestic dogs do not do this kind of play fighting and do not learn to bring down large prey as a pack.

113

Wolves are very inquisitive and must constantly monitor their home territory to detect intruders or new prey. Thus, they are very aware of changes in their territory, much like wild horses are spooked by a broken tree or other disturbance by man in their territories. Wolves raised in captivity and kept as pets exhibit this curiosity and activity in several ways. If kept in a large, comfortable outdoor enclosure, a wolf can seem content. However, they are easily frightened, defensive or aggressive if sudden intense stimuli such as a loud noise, new objects or an unfamiliar person carrying a package is introduced to their "territory". And, wolves' inquisitive nature results in pet wolves constantly searching his home – digging holes in soft surfaces – carpets, chairs and sofas. (16) Whereas a domestic dog can lie around a house all day, content to eat and sleep the day away. This lack of inquisitiveness by domestic dogs certainly works against them when they are in the wild.

Dogs have been domesticated and selectively bred for many centuries. Much of this selection has worked against domestic dogs' ability to work as a unit in the wild. For example, "In some dog breeds – especially terrier breeds – we find that selective breeding has lowered their threshold for aggression and they are not very tolerant of each other. Indeed, in a social group of five or six wire-haired fox terriers, fighting may result in the death of one or more low-ranking dogs, so that such breeds cannot be housed together in large numbers... In other breeds, such as the beagle, the 'pack instinct' seen in the wolf has also been modified; whereas the wolf pack is allegedly a closed social group which will usually repel and rarely accept strangers, the beagle pack will invariably accept additions to the pack. (17) The beagle instinct would also work against the success of the pack in the wild.

One more. Wolf mothers molt the hair on their chests and bellies and use it to build a comfortable nest for newborns. Dogs no longer molt at the time of birth. A small thing, but one more setback for dogs trying to make it on their own.

For whatever reason, dogs have not established any permanent populations in the United States. Throughout our history, there have been strays and scavengers, but no packs that have lasted more than a few generations. This does not mean that the total number of dogs living as strays has been small. There have been millions of stray dogs in the United States since about 1800. The more people, the more stray dogs. It only means that no dog packs have stayed in a natural state over enough generations to develop a distinct breed through natural selection. In some countries, such as Mexico and India, a large human population, coupled with a great deal of un-covered refuse has led to the development of pariah dogs that breed very true. (18)

The number of stray dogs has been growing as the population of the United States has grown. There are more wild, stray dogs in the United States today than there have ever been. Ironically, the animal that is considered a family's child, brother or best friend and almost held as highly as a family member is a dangerous carnivore. Much of the damage to livestock and, in fact, deaths of humans is given little thought due to the status of dogs as pets. The stories in newspapers about dogs killing people normally end with a quote from the owner or a neighbor that goes something like this: "they seemed like good dogs, never gave anyone any trouble.....I fed them sometimes."

CURRENT POPULATION AND PROBLEMS

There are no extensive, accurate surveys of the number of stray dogs in the United States today. There is complete agreement that there are stray dogs in every State, from Maine to California. A conservative estimate would put the number of stray dogs at 5 to 10 million today. Counting dogs running without a leash, the number might be 30 million. (19) Almost no effort is made to systematically remove stray dogs from our society. It would be prohibitively expensive. Animal control agencies are severely underfunded. Special efforts are made by law enforcement or natural resources officers in the case of large livestock kills or when enough complaints are lodged against packs of dogs running loose in a given area. Even when humans are attacked and killed, the number of wild dogs held accountable is minimal, for fear of a backlash among the public for killing "innocent" stray dogs.

Stray dogs have a litany of offenses against society that go essentially un-noticed because of their status as family pets. Stray dogs have a significant impact on wildlife, including deer, elk, pheasants, quail, turkeys, rabbits and other small game (20). They have taken the place of wolves as the animal causing the greatest loss of livestock in the United States – estimates range from 30 to 100 million dollars in damage each year. Stray dogs are often ill-fed and susceptible to rabies.

Every society has its absurdities. Our reaction to dogs killing people is one of our absurdities. What if they were wolves? The only reaction would be to eliminate them from proximity to humans, which seemed like a rational reaction to an animal that threatened human lives in the 1800's. Now, the first reaction when a dog kills a person is often, "What did they do with the dog?" Meaning, "I hope they didn't needlessly kill the dog without giving it a chance for re-habilitation" or, "If they had to kill the dog, I hope they did it humanely." And concern is expressed that one bad dog doesn't give the whole breed a bad name. We live in a society that finds nothing wrong with aggressive, large (impossible to control if angered) dogs living inside the confined space of homes with small children – a completely unnatural situation for the dog and one that tempts acting out by the animal. Forgotten is the fact that even the tamest domestic animal is still more wild than tame. No wonder that one-third of all insurance liability claims are from dog bites. (21)

HOUSE CATS

THE ARRIVAL OF HOUSE CATS

The only other family pet to go wild in the United States was that other carnivore -- the house cat. The ability of house cats to control mice and rats made them especially attractive to settlers in America. Cats were commonly boarded on ships to keep the ship free of mice and rats. House cats were so commonly kept by the Pilgrims that they were certainly brought to the United States on the Mayflower, yet no mention was made of them on the ship's inventory. Why would they be? Putting a house cat on the inventory would be like mentioning that some men brought a pipe and some women brought a dress.

HOW THEY BEHAVE IN THE WILD

House cats, or domestic cats, are related to the Wildcats that still live in Africa, Europe, southwest and central Asia into India, China and Mongolia. The European Wildcat is called *Felis silvestris silvestris.* The African Wildcat is *Felis silvestris lybica.* Our domestic cat is called *Felis silvestris catus.* The three types can inter-breed.

The house cat is thought to have been domesticated over 10,000 years ago. Surprisingly, it has not changed very much from the appearance and behavior of its wild ancestors. The house cat has become capable of living with humans, while the wildcat remains very wary and fearful of humans. House cats are prized as companion animals. Other than that, they remain very similar to the wildcat. They have similar skeletal shapes, similar over-all size, similar coats, similar vocalizations and similar hunting patterns. Of course, house cats have been bred to many different colors, while the wildcat is normally pale yellow to medium brown with the typical black stripes or spots of a tabby cat.

House cats have lost much of their fear of humans, which is about the only thing that distinguishes them from wild cats. However, even European wild cats will not avoid the proximity of humans and often lives not only close to settlements but even in granaries, baras, attics, summer houses, and larger residences. (22)

European wild cats live in abandoned burrows of badgers, foxes, and other animals; hollowed out trees, when the hollow is near the ground; rock crevices; or secluded nests in tall vegetation. They seldom make their own burrows or hollows.

House cats prefer to spend time in similar places -- secluded parts of a home – a dark closet, under or behind furniture, a quiet room away from people, for example. When they escape and become strays, house cats live in the same places as wild cats.

"The wildcat (hunts at dusk and dawn and sometimes into the night). It usually sets out to hunt an hour or two before sunset and remains active throughout the evening and the first half of night, then rests, and reappears again only at dawn. In summer, however, it also hunts during the day. The stomachs of cats caught two hours before sunset contained freshly caught rodents. Many cases are known, when cats have stolen domestic fowl during the day and have been encountered by hunters. The wildcat is less cautious and fearful than other animals. It will permit a man on horseback to approach within 30 to 40 paces, after which it runs away unhurriedly. It swims well but avoids water when avoiding danger. A trapped cat rumbles and hisses at an approaching man but does not attack. A captive animal is very malicious and does not become accustomed to man; taming kittens is difficult indeed. According to observations made in the Caucasus, it invariably lives and hunts alone." (23)

Except for the comment about distrust of man, this description of the wild cats' hunting habits could be talking about a stray or active outdoors domestic cat.

"In pursuing prey, sometimes the wild cat climbs to the very top of high trees, even jumping from one tree to another. It lies in wait for a prey and catches it by executing a few leaps. Sometimes it lies in wait standing (lying) near a burrow or crevice among rocks. Its leaps can reach a span of 10 feet. The cat relies on vision and audition in searching for prey. Olfaction is relatively weakly developed." (24)

This sounds like a description of a house cat stalking and catching a mouse.

"If the prey is small, the cat grabs it in its claws and then kills it by piercing the neck or back of the head. Small rodents (mice, voles, and rats) constitute their primary food everywhere; birds (chickens, ducks, and more rarely song birds) occupy second place, followed by dormice and hare. The predator hunts other animals in years of low population of mouse-like rodents, or incidentally." (25)

The prey of a stray or outdoor domestic cat is the same.

It is notable that domestication of house cats is much less apparent than for domestic dogs. The house cat "has been described as 'an exploitive captive' and a 'carnivore that enjoys the company of man'. The cat is neither a man-made species like the dog, nor simply an animal made captive for utilitarian purposes, like the elephant.

"The stable and organized social structure evident in groups of feral cats, genetically almost identical to house cats, demonstrates that association with man has little altered the cat's wild behavior patterns...Patterns of predatory behavior are practiced from an early age by kittens, and are used to considerable effect by adults; in most breeds of dogs the predatory sequence is incomplete." (26)

FROM THE EARLY COLONIES UNTIL TODAY

Not much has changed for stray house cats since they arrived in the Colonies. They fill the same niche, hunt the same prey. The differences involve human's perception of the value and place of stray cats. In the early years when most people in the United States lived on farms and were supported by agriculture, stray cats were valued for controlling mice and rats in the farm buildings. Dairy farmers usually left some milk for the mother cat and kittens to encourage them to stay on the farm. If the population of stray cats got too large, a few were shot or otherwise dispatched. Today, there is more concern for the welfare of the stray cat population but also a concern about stray cats' impact on wildlife.

House cats are not capable of living in the wild in the United States. While they maintain nearly all of the genetic and behavioral patterns of their wild ancestors, they cannot compete with foxes, coyotes and other native animals. Yet, there are an estimated 30 million "wild" house cats at the present time and probably have been a similar population of stray cats for over 150 years. Some estimates go as high as 80 million. These millions of house cats live in an ecological niche that is created by human activities. They live in urban areas where humans have driven out other predators. They live on farms where humans have built barns and other buildings that protect the house cat from predators. They may feed on rodents that are attracted by spilled grain or other by-products of human activity. They also feed on small birds and other animals that would otherwise be hunted by foxes, coyotes, etc. Some of these escaped or abandoned house cats can live for generations without interaction with humans, but they must have a house, a barn, a warehouse, a golf course, or some human activity to remove predators from their territory. (27)

House cats have become companion animals, if sometimes reluctant companions. Much like that other companion animal, the wild mustang, free-living house cats are a nuisance and have little economic value. But, since they are seen as companion animals there are highly emotional conflicts about how they should be treated.

One benefit of wild house cats is that they can reduce the population of rodents on a farm or in an urban environment. However, this benefit is counterbalanced by the potential for transmitting rabies and other diseases to humans; preying on native birds, mammals, reptiles and amphibians; fouling yards with feces; yowling and fighting at night; and leaving muddy footprints on cars and porches. These are non-native species, introduced by Europeans and dependent on humans for space to live. In a country that spends tens of millions of dollars each year to return wild areas to pristine native conditions, the first impulse would seem to be to remove them from the environment. But since house cats are companion animals, nothing about their treatment is simple.

There are numerous articles and books published each year about the plight of the wild house cat. There are several organizations dedicated to the proper treatment of wild house cats. Most towns have Animal Control Agencies that sometimes catch wild house cats. What to do with them? Trap, euthanize? Trap, Neuter and Return? Trap, Neuter and Relocate? Truly wild house cats are seldom candidates for adoption. Veterinarians and Animal Scientists disagree on the best approach. (28)

One thing is certain. Much like wild hogs and dogs, there are too many wild house cats in too many places to eliminate them all. And there are too many wild house cats for current approaches to have a major impact on them. It is understandable that there is a concern about the welfare of wild house cats, since their cousins are family pets. But the amount of effort compared to the actual results might be questioned. Only a very small percentage of wild house cats are helped by these organized efforts.

CONTACTS

For information on stray house cats:

1. Alley Cat Allies

2. Humane Society of the United States

3. Numerous state and local organizations

For information about stray dogs:

1. Humane Society of the United States

2. Numerous state and local organizations

3. Animal Rescue Leagues

CHAPTER SEVEN -- THE LOWLY BURRO. TOO COOL TO CHANGE

The donkeys get no respect; they came on Columbus' second voyage; introduced through Mexico to Texas; wild herds established in arid, remote parts of the West; behavior in the wild; used as pack animals and sires for mules in the East, no record of going wild in Colonies; famous donkeys; a donkey discovers a silver mine; efforts to preserve wild donkeys

Burro, donkey or ass. The names refer to the same animal. Whatever he is called, the donkey has stayed consistent and steadfast over time. He is the one domestic animal that has remained most constant in coloring and form, even when he escapes to the wild.

Other domestic animals have changed dramatically after generations in the wild. Not the donkey. He knows what works and he sticks with it.

It has been over 80 years since the donkey has been an economic asset in developed countries. Since about 1930 the donkey has been kept as a pet or a curiosity, but not required to do any real work. Prior to the development of machine power, the donkey was vital to the economic life of most countries in the world. Subsistence farmers relied upon the donkey for transportation, packing a variety of materials and tilling the soil. The donkey was his most valuable possession. It was said, "If the donkey dies, we will all starve".

Donkeys were domesticated before the dawn of recorded history. They played an important part in the history of all early civilizations and religions. Jesus and Mohamed were both said to ride a donkey at important times of their lives. (1)

Until recent times, the donkey was highly valued as a pack animal in the United States. Many of the advances of the 18th and 19th centuries were made on the back of the donkey. They worked in mines when other animals were too big or too skittish to do the work. They packed provisions for the building of the Transcontinental Railroad. Their hybrid offspring, the mule, was the preferred animal to pull wagon trains and cargo wagons throughout the West. The prospector and his donkey were a symbol of the discovery of gold and other minerals in all parts of the United States. Many homesteads in the North, South, East and West were built on faith, hope and the back of a donkey. (2)

Despite the donkey's obvious value, it has been the butt of jokes throughout history. The donkey's long ears, general appearance, unusual bray and cautious (some say stubborn) attitude are often ridiculed – sometimes by the same person that depends on it for subsistence. But it keeps plodding along.

And, of course, the donkey sometimes escaped to the wild in the United States. Or perhaps "wandered slowly away" would be a more apt description. They found a niche in the more arid and remote regions of the American West and remain wild there today.

INTRODUCTION INTO MEXICO AND THE SOUTHWEST

As with the other domestic animals, there were no donkeys in the Western Hemisphere before their introduction by Spanish explorers.

As if to underline the importance of the donkey to life in the 1400's, Christopher Columbus included some donkeys on his second voyage to Hispaniola in 1494. The donkey was among the important domestic animals to change life in the Western Hemisphere.

It is thought that the first donkeys to arrive in Mexico were brought by Juan de Zumarraga in 1528. (3) Zumarraga was the first Catholic Bishop in New Spain (Mexico). After seeing the poor treatment of native Indians in Mexico, Zumarraga recommended that the King of Spain send more burros to Mexico to relieve the burden on the Indians. By 1550, burros were plentiful in Mexico.

The first burros to enter the United States came with the expedition of Juan de Onate in 1598. (4) From 1600 to 1900, donkeys were used as pack animals in the desert Southwest and West of the United States. They specialized in packing supplies for prospectors and working the mines in the West. Some of the donkeys escaped to the wild and remained wild for 300 years.

Being the "lowly burro", there are few recorded observations or studies of the populations of wild donkeys in early America. It was often noted that there were wild donkeys here and there, but they didn't receive the attention that was given to the Mustang and Longhorn by historians, painters or biographers. It is thought that there were fewer wild donkeys than horses or cows. The reasons for the smaller populations of wild donkeys remain somewhat speculative.

Several factors may have accounted for the smaller populations of wild donkeys. Donkeys were not raised in large domestic herds so the numbers available to escape were naturally smaller than the horse or cow. Native Indians did not have much use for donkeys, so the Indians did not spread donkeys in the way that they spread horses throughout the West. Draft horses and oxen, rather than donkeys, were used by European settlers for cultivating the land as they moved west. Being smaller, the donkey may not have been able to defend itself against the cougar and the wolf.

Donkeys did not go wild in Florida, the Southeast or the Eastern United States. The donkey-horse hybrid, the mule, was widely used in the eastern United States, however. George Washington was one of the first to breed the large Mammoth mule, which was sometimes the preferred mount in battle. (5) Mules were the main barge animal on the Erie Canal. But the mule is sterile, thus limiting the number of donkey/mule escapees to the wild in the East.

Still, donkeys did run wild in niche areas of the West and Southwest for several centuries. They did not become a specific breed that was coveted by man, like the Mustang and Longhorn. Instead, they became a somewhat consistent type that has continually been mixed with introduced types over the years. Most wild burros today are rusty brown, brown or gray-brown with white noses. But there are mixes of black and other colors. Most have the typical cross-like pattern of dark hair on the back. Wild donkeys are generally the standard size – a medium size donkey. (6)

It could be said that the wild donkey continued to be just an ordinary donkey, instead of changing very much. Apparently the donkey was already adapted to the new environment of the Western United States when it was introduced or he was too cool to change.

HOW THEY BEHAVE IN THE WILD

Donkeys were at home in the American Southwest and West as soon as they arrived in 1598. They thrived in the arid and remote parts of the country. As wild Mustangs were driven from the more fertile areas of the west by ranchers and farmers, they began to share the same remote regions as the donkeys. Today, the donkey is found in the areas that are not preferred by the horse – areas of extreme drought and nearly unpalatable plants.

Even though donkeys and horses can be cross-bred in captivity, they do not breed in the wild. Bands of horses and donkeys occupy separate territories in the wild.

Wild donkeys have excellent eyesight and hearing (big ears). They can go without water longer than any animal except the camel. They are naturally cautious and slow to get into dangerous situations. They can eat almost anything but will avoid some poisonous plants that are harmful to horses. Donkeys can thrive on low-protein plants that are not eaten by horses, cattle, buffalo or pigs. (7)

Donkeys are wary. They can detect predators sooner than other animals and take evasive action. Donkeys make good sentinels for sheep because of this attribute. But only if there are no sheep dogs around – donkeys do not like dogs.

The slow, sedentary donkey becomes a vicious fighter if provoked by a wolf or other predator. Weighing 600 pounds or more, wild donkeys can defend themselves against predators. (8)

Much like horses, dominant male donkeys claim a territory and defend it. However, unlike horses, female donkeys may not remain as faithful to the dominant male or the territory. In some reported social groupings of wild donkeys, female donkeys wander freely between territories, often in loosely affiliated groups of 3 or 4 other females and foals. In other reports, the females stay closely affiliated with the dominant male's territory. (9)

Subordinate male donkeys do not appear to be as outcast as their horse counterparts. Some dominant males tolerate the presence of subordinate males who, in turn, help defend the territory. Subordinate males will sometimes mate with females of the same territory.

Some bachelor male donkeys roam in groups of other subordinate male donkeys. The passing of the torch to a new dominant male occurs with fights similar to horses, but without as much drama and noise.

Donkeys live longer than other domestic animals. Their life span in the wild is estimated to be 40 to 50 years. A female donkey has one foal each year for 25 to 30 years. There has never been a recorded instance of a donkey having twins. (10)

FAMOUS DONKEYS

Two classics of Spanish literature contribute to an appreciation of the donkey's character and value to humans. Don Quixote rides a donkey on his ill-fated quest. The lyric poet Juan Ramon Jimenez writes of his donkey, Platero, in a series of short tales in *Platero and I*, An Andalusian Elegy, published in 1914.

Here are two passages from *Platero and I* which illustrate the high regard that Jimenez had for his companion, his transportation and his confidante, Platero:

The Thorn

As he came into the pasture of Los Caballos, Platero began to limp. I dropped to the ground…

"But, man, what's the matter?"

Platero held his right forefoot slightly raised showing its wound, weak and limp, its hoof hardly touching the burning sand of the soil.

With greater solicitude, no doubt, than that of old Darbon, his doctor, I bent his foot and looked at his red wound. A long green thorn, from a healthy orange tree, was stuck in it like a tiny, round emerald dagger. Shaken by Platero's suffering, I pulled out the thorn; then I led the poor thing to the stream of the yellow iris so that the running water might lick his tiny wound with its long pure tongue.

Later, we moved on towards the white sea, I walking ahead, he behind, still limping and nudging me softly on the back… (11)

The Little Cart

In the large stream, which the rain had swollen up to the vineyard, we found an old little cart stuck, wholly lost beneath its load of grass and oranges. A little girl, her clothes torn and dirty, was crying by one of the wheels, trying to help with the push of her little, budding chest a smaller donkey, much smaller, oh! And thinner than Platero.

And the little donkey was struggling against the wind, trying in vain to pull the cart from the mud, at each sobbing cry of the little girl. His effort was in vain, as that of courageous children, as the flight of those tired summer breezes, that fall, in a faint among the flowers.

I gave Platero a little pat and, as best as I could, I hitched him to the little cart in front of the pitiful donkey. I forced him, then, with a loving command, and Platero, in one pull, dragged the little cart and the donkey from the hole in the mud and pulled them up the slope.

What smiles on the little girl's face! It was as if the evening sun, while setting among rain clouds, and breaking in yellow crystals, was lighting up a dawn behind her soiled tears.

In her weeping joy, she offered me two choice oranges, delicate, heavy, round. I took them, grateful, and then I gave one to the weak little donkey, as sweet consolation; the other, to Platero, as golden prize. (12)

THE JACK-ASS OF THE COEUR d'ALENES

Numerous tall tales are associated with the donkeys who accompanied miners in the American West. The most famous donkey -- brought to life in magazines, newspapers, books and gossip -- was the donkey credited with discovering the Bunker Hill and Sullivan mines in the Coeur d'Alene Mountains of northern Idaho.

This is a summary of the story found in *Asses vs. Jackasses* by William G. Long, pp. 51-62:

There was a dispute about who discovered the fabulously rich silver and lead mine that became known as the Bunker Hill and Sullivan mine. Two prospectors, O'Rourke and Kellogg, were in some kind of arrangement

131

with two businessmen from Murray, Idaho named Cooper and Peck. When the mine was discovered and the extent of the riches became known, O'Rourke and Kellogg cut Cooper and Peck out of the deal.

Cooper and Peck sued and the case made it to the Idaho State Supreme Court. The Supreme Court's decision was written by Judge Norman Buck. He wrote, in part, "From the evidence of witnesses, this Court is of the opinion that the Bunker Hill mine was discovered by the jackass, Phil O'Rourke, and N.S. Kellogg; and as the jackass is the property of the plaintiffs, Cooper and Peck, they are entitled to a half-interest in the Bunker Hill and a quarter interest in the Sullivan claims."

So, since Cooper and Peck had provided O'Rourke and Kellogg with materials, including a donkey, for their search and were otherwise in a business relationship with each other, the judge gave part ownership to the men who provided the grubstake for the prospectors.

However, one part of the decision was taken out of context to became the root of endless tall tales. The phrase "was discovered by the jackass" gave the donkey much more than its due.

Soon, there were detailed stories about how the donkey had come across the mine. The donkey had seen the silver glistening in the sun across a valley; the donkey had run away from camp and come across the mine; the donkey got one fourth of the mines earnings and retired a millionaire; the donkey spent his money on chewing tobacco and liquor and died from drinking too much moonshine. All these stories swirled around the donkey.

Whatever the truth of the matter, more was written and discussed about the jackass of the Bunker Hill and Sullivan Mines than any other prospector's donkey of the West.

CURRENT STATUS OF WILD DONKEYS IN AMERICA

Wild donkeys are protected by the 1971 Wild Free-Roaming Horses and Burros Act. This act requires the Bureau of Land Management to protect the donkeys and maintain an acceptable population in the wild.

The Bureau of Land Management estimates that there are 5,500 wild donkeys today. (13) Nearly all of them are in California, Arizona and Nevada. The BLM sets an Acceptable Management Level and tries to find adoptive homes for the excess donkeys. This system is meant to preserve the current population of wild donkeys without undo damage to the habitat.

BREED ASSOCIATIONS, PRESERVATION ORGANIZATIONS

The wild burro is not a registered breed. It is listed as a minor breed in some publications.

There are no organizations exclusively dedicated to the preservation of wild burros. There are several organizations that support the preservation of wild mustangs and wild burros, but the burros play second fiddle to the mustangs.

In the present-day United States donkeys are bred for pleasure, with color and size being the traits of interest. Little value is placed on wild donkeys' potential as a genetic source for disease resistance, endurance, speed or ability to thrive on little water and nourishing food. These traits are not sought by breeders of domestic donkeys in the United States.

Somewhere in Kentucky there may be a thoroughbred horse breeder who is dreaming of finding the next

Secretariat genes in a herd of wild Mustangs.   There is probably nobody dreaming about the genes of wild donkeys.

CONTACTS AND BLM AREAS

To locate herds of wild burros:

1. BLM's Wild Horse and Burro Program National Program Office

2. The American Mustang and Burro Association

3. The American Donkey and Mule Society

CHAPTER EIGHT – THE HAWAIIAN "BARNYARD"; COW ISLANDS OF ALASKA

Cattle brought to Hawaii by George Vancouver; cattle went wild and flourished on all the islands; John Parker brings wild cattle under control and establishes the Parker Ranch; other farm animals arrive and cause immense ecological damage; efforts to reduce damage from well-established farm animals in the wild of Hawaii; cattle introduced to numerous islands in Southwest Alaska; government efforts to establish a competitive local cattle industry; the final herd of cattle on Chirikof Island

HAWAII

The only domestic animals on Hawaii prior to contact with Europeans were the chicken and a small Polynesian pig. Much of the protein in the native Hawaiian diet came from fish. (1)

Europeans brought cattle, horses, sheep, goats, donkeys, swine, house cats, dogs and new varieties of chickens to the islands. Each of these domestic animals – except horses -- has run wild in sizeable populations at one time or another. Hawaii has a year-round climate that supports their life in the wild. Even sheep are able to live in this tropical paradise, free of the predators that prevented them from surviving in the wild of the mainland U.S. Native Hawaiians and preservationists sometimes refer to this over-abundance of farm animals living in the wild as "Hawaii's barnyard".

CATTLE

Cattle were introduced to the Hawaiian Islands 250 years after they had come to the mainland United States. In 1793 George Vancouver, a British explorer, picked up 6 cows and a bull from the Spanish mission in Monterey, California and brought them by ship to Hawaii. (2) They were solid red and solid black Spanish-type cattle. The cattle were to be gifts to curry favor with the ruling class in Hawaii. The native Hawaiians of the time had little contact with the Western world. At the time of Vancouver's journey the Hawaiian natives were sometimes hostile, other times friendly. Vancouver thought that cattle would be accepted as a major offering of friendship. He expected that the Hawaiians would immediately recognize the value of this new animal.

Vancouver planned to present the cattle to King Kamehameha on the Big Island of Hawaii. This was prior to

Kamehameha's unification of the Hawaiian Islands. Because of poor rations and stifling heat on board ship, several of the cows died before landing. The lone bull also died after delivery. Vancouver was determined that cattle be introduced to Hawaii and brought more cows and 3 bulls to the island in 1794. (3) He asked Kamehameha to order that anyone who killed cattle would face the death penalty. The King agreed and put the order in place for ten years. In this way, the cattle thrived and multiplied. The order was not lifted until 1830. By this time cattle had escaped to the wilder parts of the island and flourished. It was estimated that tens of thousands of wild cattle roamed the hills, valleys and mountains of Hawaii along with many semi-wild cattle from ranches on the plains. (4)

The predecessors of the Hawaiian cattle were likely pure Spanish. They had come from Andalusia in Spain, to the Indies, to Mexico, to California and now to Hawaii. In physical appearance they resembled the Andalusian cattle and the Florida Cracker cow.

The founder of the well-known Parker Ranch on Hawaii, John Parker, settled in Hawaii in 1815. Parker was one of the few foreigners that the King allowed to stay in Hawaii. When Parker arrived, Kamehameha's wild cattle were becoming a nuisance. One of the first tasks assigned to Parker was to shoot wild cattle and reduce their population near towns to keep the wild cattle from destroying native crops. (5)

Because of the numerous ravines and canyons on the islands, wild cattle in Hawaii were particularly dangerous. As a person walked into a ravine, the cattle appeared to be trapped. When cornered, cattle usually attacked.

King Kamehameha recognized that the cattle could have economic value if they could be rounded up or increased on large ranches. The land and climate were favorable for his plan but he did not have laborers who were trained to hunt or handle cattle. He invited cowboys from California – Anglos, Indians, Mexican and Spanish – to come to Hawaii for employment. This colorful set of cowboys had all of the skill needed to turn the wild cattle of Hawaii into a profitable business. These cowboys also taught native Hawaiians to handle cattle. The imported Spanish-speaking cowboys and their native students became known as the "paniolos" – a take-off of the word Espanol. These paniolos remain a colorful part of Hawaiian culture today. (6)

From about 1815 to 1840 the main activity of the paniolos was to hunt and kill wild cattle or round them up to be driven to a sea-side market. Trade in hides and tallow from wild cattle helped stabilize the reign of King Kamehameha III. Many sailing shipped stopped on the island to replenish supplies of salted beef. (7)

The thrilling hunt of the Paniolos was captured by writer Isabella Bird:

"I sat for an hour on horseback on a rocky hill while they hunted in the woods. Then I heard the deep voices of bulls, and a great burst of cattle appeared, with hunters in pursuit, but the herd vanished over a dip of the hillside and the natives joined me.

Putting our horses into a gallop we dashed down the hill till we were close up with the chase; then another tremendous gallop, and a brief wild rush, the grass shaking with the surge of cattle and horses. There was much whirling of tails and tearing up of the earth – a lasso spun three or four times around the head of the native who rode in front of me, and almost simultaneously a fine red bullock lay prostrate on the earth, nearly strangled, with his foreleg noosed to his throat. The other natives dismounted, and put two lassoes round his horns, slipping the first into the same

*position, and vaulted into their saddles before he was on his
legs.*

*He got up, shook himself, put his head down, and
made a mad blind rush, but his captors were too dexterous
for him, and in that and each succeeding rush he was foiled.
As he tore wildly from side to side, the natives dodged under
the lasso, slipping it over their heads, and swung themselves
over their saddles, hanging in one stirrup, to aid their trained
horses to steady themselves as the bullock tugged violently
against them."(8)*

The Parker Ranch was established officially in 1847.
The Parker Ranch eventually imported Hereford cattle and
phased out the Spanish breeds. The ranch is still one of the
largest in the United States. It consists of several thousand
acres on the Big Island, producing more than 30,000 beef
cattle each year.

There are very few wild cattle in Hawaii today. The
remaining small population of wild Spanish cattle could only
be found in the wildest parts of the highest elevations. They
evolved into a Spanish-type breed that was relatively small
in size. They came to be referred to as "Old Vancouvers",
after the man who brought them to the Islands. Old
Vancouvers were normally solid red or solid black in color.
They were the common Criollo conformation. Over the
years, escapees of other breeds had joined the wild herd
and mixed with them. The last few wild cattle in the most
remote parts of the island of Hawaii were mixed colors and
forms, particularly showing some Hereford traits.

Old Vancouvers had a sentimental following due to
their impact on the history of the Islands. In an effort to
preserve the breed, several wild cattle were kept at the
Honolulu Zoo in 1969. These specimens were quite variable
in color and form.

More recently, groups supporting the preservation of Hawaii's natural habitat have made a strong case that all of the non-native domestic animals cause unacceptable damage to the ecosystems of the islands. The few remaining wild cattle have very little public support for their preservation.

WILD HOGS

Captain James Cook brought domestic swine to Hawaii in 1778. As with cattle, they were given a 10-year grace period to become established. The larger European swine quickly hybridized with the smaller Polynesian varieties or replaced them altogether. The imported pigs multiplied so rapidly that foresters and land owners tried to eliminate them in the late 1800's. Fencing, poisoning, hunting and bounties kept the population under control during the early 20th century. (9)

Sport hunting became popular in Hawaii after World War II. One of the most coveted game animals was the wild hog. In the 1950's, the responsibility for controlling the wild hog population in Hawaii was transferred to the Department of Land and Natural Resources. A system of hunting permits and quotas was set up to maintain the population of wild pigs at a targeted level, rather than eliminating them completely.

In recent years, as more environmental damage is reported, the DLNR target level population of wild pigs has come under question.

WILD GOATS AND SHEEP

Goats and sheep are even more destructive of native habitat than cattle and hogs. Both of these domestic animals were introduced to Hawaii prior to 1780. They both have established wild populations in niche habitats on the islands.

Recent efforts to completely remove goats and sheep from designated areas have been successful. Fencing and shooting by volunteers have been cost-effective. It is likely that the program will eliminate all wild goats and sheep except for animals maintained in hunting preserves. (10)

WILD DONKEYS

Donkeys were also introduced to Hawaii. Donkeys get no respect, so there is no record of when they came to the islands. But they did come and some of them escaped to live in rural areas. Donkeys never have had a large population in Hawaii, but they do become a nuisance now and then. The wild donkeys sometimes find their way into urban areas and damage gardens, landscaping and structures.

Over the years there have been some roundups of the donkeys. Some have been sent to the mainland U.S. for adoption and others have been quietly disposed of.

WILD DOMESTIC DOGS

Hawaiians had small dogs for centuries before Europeans arrived, much like they had small pigs. These small dogs were often fed well and served as ritual food during ceremonies, in addition to being family and personal pets. (11)

When Europeans brought new breeds of dogs to the Islands, many of them escaped and lived in the wild in a similar manner to the mainland. However, without predators, dogs became a greater problem in Hawaii than in the mainland. They were such a problem that eradication programs were needed to bring the populations under control in the 1800's. (12)

Today, most of the wild dogs in Hawaii are strays that move between their domestic homes and the outlying areas of the islands. Dogs are used as sporting animals for wild hog hunting and some of them stay behind. While packs of wild dogs are not widespread on the islands, each year there are dog bites and more serious attacks reported.

WILD DOMESTIC CATS

Domestic cats came to Hawaii with the early Europeans. They soon escaped and established a wild population in all parts of the islands.

Domestic animals are more wild than tame – even cats. Nobody knows the number of wild cats in Hawaii, but there are a lot of them. On the mainland of the United States, the population and distribution of wild house cats is controlled by predators such as coyotes and foxes. There are no such predators in Hawaii. Wild cats live in forested areas where they prey on native and non-native birds. Cats are nocturnal. They can catch birds in their roosts at night. (13) They certainly have an impact on bird populations on the islands, but the impact is difficult to measure. The Hawaiian state bird is not threatened by the wild house cats because most of the Nene's habitat will not support wild house cats.

Like wild hogs, it would be very difficult to eradicate all of the wild cats in Hawaii.

COW ISLANDS OF ALASKA

Cattle were pastured on the Aleutian Islands of Alaska in the early 1900s, much like domestic animals were pastured on Atlantic Coast islands in colonial times. The Aleutian Islands were used as cow pastures in an attempt to establish a local source of beef in Alaska. Improvements in the efficient transport of beef from the lower forty-eight states eliminated the demand for locally-produced beef. Some wild cattle roamed the islands for several decades after the local farms went out of business. U.S. Fish and Wildlife Service eventually removed the cattle from all of the islands except Chirikof. (14)

The wild cattle were not removed from Chirikof Island due to confusion over the ownership of the cattle and the island. (15) Also, there were individuals and groups who wanted the Chirikof herd to remain because there had been cattle on Chirikof longer than anyone could remember. The historical record is fairly clear that cattle have been on Chirikof Island since the mid- to late 1800s. Siberian cattle may have been introduced to Chirikof and other Aleutian islands by the Russians as early as 1794. (16) It is thought that someone (maybe Russians, maybe not) brought the cattle to the island to set up a business of selling meat to whaling crews. The cattle were abandoned and persisted in a population of 800 to 1000 cows despite the island's barren vegetation, challenging climate and lack of human attention.

Chirikof Island is about 80 miles southwest of Kodiak Island, Alaska. The island consists of 28,000 acres. It has no trees. Grasses and sedges eke out a fragile existence on the island. The cattle survive on the native grasses and other plants. They sometimes eat kelp that washes up on shore. Chirikof Island has had human inhabitants on and off but currently has no permanent residents. The weather is not extreme, by Alaska standards. That is why the Aleutians were chosen for the fledgling cattle industry in the first place. The Aleutian Islands are warmed by the Japanese current. There are some slight hills and ridges on Chirikof that provide shelter for the cattle. The average low winter temperature is about 25 degrees Fahrenheit at Kodiak, the nearest weather station. The all-time record low temperature was minus 16 degrees F. These are very similar readings to Kansas City, Kansas. (17) So, it is not astonishing to find cattle that survive these temperatures. The sea surrounding Chirikof Island is often wind-whipped and travel to the island is difficult. There are dangerous reefs around the island making it difficult to access the island by boat. There is no harbor. Rather, there is only one narrow landing beach.

What breeds of cattle are on Chirikof? These cattle were not an improved breed and no attempt to improve them was made by the Russians after they came to Chirikof. It is uncertain if any of the original Siberian cattle remained when other breeds were added to the mix. An attempt was made to utilize the islands for finishing beef cattle in the late 1800's. The name of the entrepreneur and the breeds of cattle introduced have been lost to history. In the early 1900's, Galloway cattle were introduced to Sitkalidak Island as part of a Department of Agriculture experiment. Galloways may also have been place on Chirikof. (18) Highland cattle may also have been added around this time. From the 1920's to the 1940's, the cattle on Chirikof belonged to one of the pioneers of the Alaskan frontier, Jack McCord. McCord had many business ventures in Alaska, but his passion was producing cattle on the islands. McCord introduced Hereford cattle to Chirikof. He probably introduced some Galloways, too. He gave up his interest in the cattle in 1949. (19)

Who owns them now? Over the years following McCord, there have been conflicting claims of ownership and the cattle have not been cared for. The cost of removing the cattle from an island with no harbor and vicious seas has discouraged removal of the cattle even when the title to the cattle seemed to be clear. The ownership of the island itself has been unclear. Was it the property of the State of Alaska or the U.S. Federal Government? Recently, the U.S. Federal Government has assumed ownership. As recently as 2000 the island was leased from the federal government by a private individual. When that lease expired, the land reverted to the Alaska Maritime National Wildlife Refuge.

The charter of the Wildlife Refuge is to restore the island to its natural state and protect indigenous seabirds. That would require removal of the cattle.

However, the Refuge ran into legal issues and resistance from groups that want the cattle preserved in some way. So the cattle remain on Chirikof Island today. The cattle may be a mix of the Russian originals, Herefords, Galloways, Highland and perhaps other breeds. They are not a true breeding type (yet).

To help decide the fate of the cattle, a study was commissioned to look into the genetic make-up of the Chirikof Island cattle. Were they unique enough to constitute a valuable gene pool deserving of preservation? The study concluded that "Clearly the Chirikof Island population is unique and differentiated from contemporary commercial beef germplasm widely available in North America. Thus, the Chirikof Island population represents a novel genetic resource that may be of importance for conservation and industry." (20)

If these findings are accepted by the Wildlife Refuge, perhaps the cattle will remain on Chirikof. Or, the fact that these are the only free-living cattle remaining in the United States may influence the decision.

CONTACTS AND PRESERVATION GROUPS

To inquire about Chirikof cattle:

1. Alaska Maritime Wildlife Refuge, Aleutian Islands Unit

To learn more about the Hawaiian "barnyard":

1. Hawaii Department of Land and Natural Resources

2. rarehawaii.org

CHAPTER NINE – CAMELS FROM PERSIA, AFRICA AND MONGOLIA

Popular press urges camels be brought to help cross the Western deserts; first camels arrive in Texas in 1856; U.S. Army establishes a Camel Corps; camels prove to be efficient pack animals; Civil War interrupts military camel experiment; private entrepreneurs import camels from China, Mongolia; Transcontinental Railroad eliminates need for camels; camels released to the deserts from several locations; credible sightings of wild camels in 1901; unconfirmed sightings until 1941.

In 1856, there was growing public sentiment for new ways to reach the West Coast. California had just become a state, but communication between it and the rest of the country was slow. Mail or freight could go to California in only three ways. A ship could travel to Panama, unload the cargo, cart it across the isthmus, load it on another ship which took it to California. This took 3 to 4 months. Or, a ship could travel all the way around the southern tip of South America and bring the cargo to California on a non-stop voyage. This took 6 to 8 months. Finally, lighter-weight items such as small packages and letters could travel across country. Trains and river boats could get cargo to St. Louis, but there were no navigable east-west waterways west of the Mississippi. Wagons were used between St. Louis and the west coast. This took 2 to 3 months. Most people doubted that the Transcontinental Railroad could be built and operated successfully. (1)

The public was willing to try anything that promised an improvement. It was thought that camels might be a more efficient animal to pack cargo across the deserts of the southwestern part of the country, newly won from Mexico. Other pack animals, such as mules, oxen and horses were marginally adequate for hauling cargo and mail between the new states of Texas and California. The U.S. Army was looking for a better way to carry cargo to isolated outposts in the West.

The idea of using camels to transport goods through the western desert had gained public support for 20 years before camels were finally tried. Secretary of War Jefferson Davis was instrumental in putting the plans into motion. From 1853 to 1857, he was the Secretary of War under President Pierce, before becoming the President of the Confederacy. After hearing several optimistic accounts of what the camels may be able to do, Secretary Davis asked Congress to approve the funds to purchase enough camels to allow the Army to determine whether camels would fill a practical need. (2) Secretary Davis was convinced that camels could transport cargo to far-flung military outposts in the West. Also, the dromedary camel could travel much farther without food or water than a horse. Perhaps a fleet of these camels would give the military an advantage over the Plains Indians.

Secretary Davis chose Major Henry C. Wayne and Lieutenant David D. Porter to travel to the Mideast and Africa to select the best types of camels for conditions in the desert southwest. The men studied everything they could find about camels. Wayne stopped in London to learn from experienced animal experts in England.

Wayne and Porter were instructed to purchase two types of camels – some Bactrian and some dromedaries. Bactrians were favored for packing heavy loads and the dromedaries would be tried as cavalry mounts.

Congress had appropriated adequate money to purchase only the highest quality camels. Wayne and Porter's job was to find them. On their first stop in Tunisia, they purchased one camel and were given two camels by the Monarch of Tunis. After several stops, they arrived in Constantinople (Istanbul). The Crimean War was in progress at the time. The British Army escorted them to the staging area where Wayne and Porter observed camels in service of the military. They were told that soldiers could ride a dromedary camel 70 miles a day. The dromedary could carry 600 pounds of freight 25 or 30 miles a day. The Bactrian camel could carry much more than that. (3)

Back in Constantinople, the pair learned that the Sultan of Turkey would provide them with 4 camels from his personal herd, but they would need to wait several days for them. They decided to travel on without the Turkish camels. Their next stop was in Alexandria, Egypt where they picked up 9 camels after several diplomatic starts and stops. Finally, they picked up 21 camels in Smyrna (Izmir, Turkey).

In a letter to Secretary Davis, Wayne listed all of the camels he was bringing to Texas (4):

1 Tunis camel of burden, male
1 Sennar dromedary, male
1 Muscat dromedary, female
2 Siout dromedaries, males
4 Siout dromedaries, females
1 Mount Sinai dromedary, male
2 Bactrian camels, males
1 "Booghdee" or "Tuilu", male
4 Arabian camels of burden, males
15 Arabian camels of burden, females
1 Arabian camel 24 days old, male

It can be seen from this list that Wayne was planning to have the camels reproduce in the United States. Wayne also hired some experienced camel handlers, natives of Egypt and Turkey. The Army promised them life-long employment in the United States or a free trip back to their native countries as an incentive to join the team.

CAMEL CORPS EXPERIMENTS PROVE THEIR VALUE

Major Wayne was assigned to stay with the camels after their arrival in Texas.

The camels were put ashore at Indianola, Texas (near present-day Port Lavaca) on May 14, 1856. (5) From there, Wayne took the camels to Camp Verde, a military outpost 60 miles west of San Antonio. There he built a replica of a camel stable he had seen on his voyage. The camels were well fed and recovered quickly from their ocean trip. By August, Wayne was ready to test the camels.

Wayne sent 3 wagons pulled by 6-mule teams to San Antonio to bring back 3,700 pounds of oats. As a comparison, he also sent 6 camels to bring back the same amount. They arrived in San Antonio together, as planned. Once loaded, they returned at their own pace. The mules were slowed by the heat and need for water. The camels completed the return trip 42 hours sooner than the wagons. (6)

The camels were sent on short trips with the Army cavalry and reported to be of assistance. On other trips to San Antonio for supplies, the camels were able to travel on muddy roads when wagons could not go. The initial experiments with the camels were a success.

Some difficulties with the camels were also uncovered. Some soldiers did not take to the strange animals. The behavior of camels, like any large farm animal, must be understood and accommodated, rather than confronted. Unlike horses or cattle, camels are capable of regurgitating large amounts of partially digested food and spitting it on nearby workers. If provoked, a camel is capable of biting a man's arm clean through. If taken by surprise, herds of horses, mules and donkeys can be alarmed by camels to the point of hysteria and stampede. It was going to take some time to fit camels into a routine that was established with wagons and packs carried by these other animals.

By the end of the year, Major Wayne sensed that he did not have the support of the military men at Camp Verde. Plus, Jefferson Davis was being replaced as Secretary of War. Wayne traveled back to Washington to give his final report to Davis and was finished with the camel experiment. (7)

The new Secretary of War, John B. Floyd, was enthusiastic about the potential of camels for the military and settling the Southwest. He picked Edward Fitzgerald Beale to head the experiment and immediately sent Beale on an expedition to determine the camels' worth. He was to survey the land west of Fort Defiance, New Mexico to the Colorado River and determine the best route for a wagon road (which eventually became the route for the southern branch of the Transcontinental Railroad).

Before Beale arrived at Camp Verde, 41 more camels were delivered on the second voyage of the *Supply*. These would be the last camels imported by the Army. Beale selected the best 25 camels to serve as pack animals for his surveying expedition. On June 19, 1857, the caravan of camels, mule-teams, men and horses set out on a 2,500 mile round trip. The camels would be left in California, while Beale would return to Texas the next year.

One disadvantage of the camels was quickly learned. The packs were not designed ideally and the men were not familiar with the proper way to load the packs. This caused sores on the camels. However, the camels healed quickly and this difficulty was overcome by closer supervision of the packing.

A distinct advantage for the camels was also observed. They did not rely on grass, oats or grain that needed to be packed along with the caravan. They readily ate greasewood and other shrubs along the way, basically becoming self-sustaining. And, of course, they could travel without water much further than the other animals.

By September 5 the caravan was near present-day Holbrook, Arizona. Beale wrote in his journal: *"The camels are so quiet and give us so little trouble, that sometimes we forget they are with us. Certainly there never was anything so patient and enduring and so little troublesome as this noble animal. They pack their heavy load of corn, of which they never taste a grain; put up with any food that is offered them without complaint, and are always up with the wagons, and, withal, so perfectly docile and quiet that they are the admiration of the whole camp….At this time there is not a man in the camp who is not delighted with them."* (8)

The survey was completed to the Colorado River. From there, the caravan moved on to Ft. Tejon, California where the camels were housed. Beale rode a few of the camels to Los Angeles, which created quite a stir. The following spring, Beale returned to Texas along a similar route – this time by mule train. The 25 camels remained in California where they continued to demonstrate their value as pack animals in a hot or cold desert.

Beale continued to Washington, DC and made his report to Secretary of War Floyd. Floyd requested Congress to authorize funds for 1,000 more camels. (9)   The Civil War intervened before these plans could materialize.

PRIVATE ENTREPENEURS BRING MORE CAMELS

The reports about the military camels sparked the imaginations of civilians, too. It seemed logical that camels could replace other pack animals for a profit, especially across the western United States.

A San Francisco merchant, Otto Esche, imported 45 camels – some from Mongolia and some from Siberia. He sold them to various buyers, including a mining company in British Columbia, Canada. Mrs. M. J. Watson brought 89 camels to Texas to provide transportation. After some difficulties with the port authorities, the camels were sent ashore without a permit. Some were eventually sold to a rancher who also could not find a buyer for them. He set them loose. (10) There may have been other shipments of camels to Texas that went unrecorded.

CAMELS RELEASED TO THE WILD

The Texas herd of camels stayed at Camp Verde through the Civil War. In 1863 three of the dromedaries broke away from the rest of the herd. They traveled together and were found in Arkansas by Union soldiers. They were sent by river boat to a farm on the Mississippi river in Iowa and later moved to St. Louis to be sold. (11)

After the Civil War, the Army lost interest in the camels at Camp Verde. The Transcontinental Railroad was becoming a reality and the West was becoming settled. The remaining 66 camels were sold at auction in 1866. The buyer attempted to establish a freight business between Texas and Mexico, but it was not a success. Finally, all the remaining camels were brought back to Texas and released. Most apparently headed west toward Arizona.

The mining company in British Columbia released their camels. Some of these apparently made it all the way south to Nevada and perhaps joined the herd from Arizona.

Camels from the Ft. Tejon herd in California and private entrepreneurs were either sold to zoos or circuses. Some ended up with mining companies in Nevada. The Nevada camels were used for several years but eventually all of the remaining camels were let go in the desert. In all, there were 10 or more releases of camels that resulted in a wild herd in Nevada or Arizona. (12)

It is thought that the wild camel herd was capable of reproducing and increasing its numbers in the United States. Based on the climate, there is no reason to think otherwise. Sightings of relatively young camels for several decades after their release seem to confirm that the herd did reproduce.

Numerous sightings of wild camels continued until as late as 1941. Many of the sightings were unconfirmed and some could have been merely rumor. However, some were made by authoritative sources. In January, 1896 the New York Times reported a camel killed by a Southern Pacific Railroad engine. It is hard to argue with a dead camel on the tracks. (13) In 1901 a joint United States/Mexico border commission with several military officers observed a group of wild camels, many of which were thought to be offspring of the original imported herd.

After that, it becomes less reasonable to believe reports of sightings of wild camels. The local Indian tribes killed the camels for their meat, often to mark a special occasion. Some people shot the camels for sport. If a camel broke down a fence or ate from a garden, it was hunted down. One wild camel became a local legend. See

Appendix Three for the story of the Ghost Red Camel. There are some residents near the more isolated areas of our desert who think that wild camels are still running loose.

HOW CAMELS BEHAVE IN THE WILD

Very little is known about camel's behavior in the wild. Camels were domesticated 5,000 years ago. They were so valuable to man that nearly every wild camel was captured and put to use centuries ago. The only remaining wild camels are in northern Mongolia – a herd of about 1,000 animals. This is the only herd that has never been domesticated. Due to its isolation, it has not been studied.(14)

The situation in Australia points to what might have happened if our desert area had been larger and less populated. In the mid-1800's, 12,000 camels were taken to Australia for much of the same reasons they came to the United States. In 2010 it was estimated that there were over 1 million camels in the desert of Australia.

The camels in Australia form social groups with one dominant male. Males fight (it is more like wrestling) to maintain control of a social group. Groups are moderately territorial. When resources are plentiful they share territories with other groups. In times of severe drought, groups will join together in search of water. (15)

CONTACTS

To contact groups interested in the history of camels in the U.S.:

1. The Texas Camel Corps
2. Camp Verde, Texas General Store

CHAPTER TEN – THE CHICKENS COME HOME TO ROOST

All chickens are derived by selective breeding from the Red Junglefowl; chickens cannot sustain a wild population when predators are present; chickens can escape and live in areas without their natural predators; wild chickens are often found in urban settings; urban chickens are a nuisance to some and a joy to others

There were no chickens in the United States until the European settlers brought their domestic chicken breeds here. The United States had turkeys, hawks, eagles and hundreds of song birds, but no chickens. There was a species we now call a prairie chicken, but it is actually a type of quail, not a chicken. (1)

Domestic chickens are descended from the Red Junglefowl, a native of Southeast Asia and associated islands. Domestic chickens have been selectively bred for over 10,000 years and hardly resemble the Red Junglefowl. The scientific name of the Red Junglefowl is *Gallus gallus*. The scientific name of all domestic chickens is *Gallus gallus domesticus*, indicating that the domestic chicken is still capable of inter-breeding with its ancestor species. (2)

The Red Junglefowl is capable of survival in the wild over a large area of Southeast Asia, nearby islands and several other countries where it has been introduced. It is similar to the common North American ringneck pheasant in its ability to survive.

Domestic chickens are almost incapable of survival in the wild, due to various weaknesses that have accompanied selective breeding. For example, the domestic chicken cannot fly as far as the Junglefowl; some domestic chickens do not incubate the eggs that they lay; most have lost their innate sense of fear of humans; some have lost the ability to evade predators and nearly all have lost the deadly spikes on their legs that serve as a vicious defensive and offensive weapon in a fight. (3)

Chickens are thought to have been domesticated about 7 to 8,000 B.C. It is speculated that they were first domesticated to serve as recreation – the stars of pre-historic cock fights. Red Junglefowl are still used for cock fighting in some countries today.

Domesticated chickens slowly were transported westward and found their way to Europe (Greece) by 2,000 B.C. So, Europeans had about 3,500 years to selectively breed their chickens before bringing them to the United States.

HOW THEY BEHAVED IN THE WILD

As chickens have been domesticated over the centuries, they have undergone significant changes in appearance. The Red Junglefowl male is brightly colored while the female is quite dull. There is much less difference in appearance between male and female domestic chickens. Red Junglefowl are far more cautious and wary than their domestic descendants. If only slightly disturbed, Red Junglefowl will move their roosts at least 100 yards. They will reduce their crowing for several days. Domestic chickens resume normal activities within minutes of being disturbed, as long as the disturbance appears to be over.

The foraging activity of the Red Junglefowl is very different than the domestics. The Junglefowl finds several sources of food and visits each one briefly, as if it is not certain that the source will be there tomorrow. A domestic chicken is satisfied with one food source and does not search for another.

Studies have shown that hierarchy and dominance are similar between the two types of chickens, suggesting that this instinct is very deeply ingrained. (4)

CHICKENS RUNNING WILD

Chickens have never established wild populations in any area of the United States. In fact, it may be correct to say that there are no wild chickens in the United States and never have been.

However, there are small flocks of chickens that fend for themselves, without human interference for a period of time. They are mostly in urban areas and are allowed to run loose because humans show benign neglect for a while. At any time, the chickens could be rounded up and eliminated, if people decided to do so.

Wild chickens in the United States *have* precipitated lengthy feuds between groups that want them to run free and groups that want them eliminated. In this way, they are much like the mustangs, longhorns and razorbacks – only on a much smaller, and perhaps humorous, scale.

People have probably been killed in disputes over wild chickens. How embarrassing. You can imagine the following scene:

Man arrives at the Pearly Gates after being shot in a dispute over wild chickens.

St. Peter: "Welcome to Paradise, Mr. Smith. How did you die?"

Mr. Smith: "I was shot by my neighbor."

St. Peter: "Why did he shoot you?"

Mr. Smith: "I told him to stop feeding the wild chickens. Their crowing woke me up at night."

St. Peter: "Did he stop?"

Mr. Smith: "No. He kept feeding them, so I confronted him. We got into a shouting match and one thing led to another....."

St. Peter: "So he shot you. Did you regret the things you said to him – the profanity that you used and the anger you displayed – and did you seek forgiveness as you traveled up here?"

Mr. Smith, still seething with anger: "No. I wish I had shot *him*. The SOB and his GD chickens. Is there any way I can go back and get him? I wish......"

St. Peter: "Well now. We may have to re-route you."

MODERN-DAY DISPUTES OVER CHICKENS (SEMI-WILD)

Miami, Florida -- City's Stray Chickens: Friend or Foe?
From the Miami New Times, February 23, 2010, by Erik Maza:

Until last October, the city used to pay a guy $14,000 a year to round up the thousands of stray chickens that roam our pockmarked streets. In a story in this week's *New Times*, Lesther Jorge, the last "Chicken Buster", toured some old battle sites, like Overtown, the Gaza of stray fowl.

He found that in his absence the cluckers have multiplied furiously, like Gremlins. One dilapidated tenement near Gibson Park he'd cleared back in September was overrun with the animals. "Think about it, one chicken can lay 15, 20 eggs, and maybe 10 of them will hatch," Lesther says. Even when he was actively working, he estimated he caught only 30 percent of the thousands of chicks around town. The city eliminated Chicken Busters last year in the middle of a budget crisis. Without them, what can *you* do to keep the birds at bay? A poultry expert at the University of Florida, the improbably named Gary Butcher, got all zen when asked about it: stop worrying and learn to love the chickens. "If you're talking about hens, they're less of a disturbance than dogs," he said. "They don't bark. They don't attack strangers or the mailman. We should get rid of dogs instead of chickens."

Roosters, on the other hand, might only be an inconvenience to suburbanites who like to sleep in late, Butcher said. But as far as diseases go, wild chickens are no more of a threat than squirrels. Butcher, who's got several degrees in avian virology and runs the avian disease department at the university, is an admitted chicken cheerleader. And he's noticed he's not the only one. "For some reason, it seems in the last several years people are showing more interest in chickens," he said. "I think there's this move back to nature, where people want to have farm animals as pets."

For Harry Wilcox, an avuncular 63-year-old who regularly feeds the chickens that gather behind his Overtown tenement, the benefits are more tangible. "Eggs," he said. "You gotta go in the bushes and look for them, but the eggs are good."

Key West, Florida -- Feral Cats and Chickens of the Conch Republic
From Encyclopedia Brittanica, Advocacy for Animals, online, August 18, 2008

... the legion of colourful chickens that stroll the streets, camp out in back yards, and loll about in restaurants and taverns. Some 2,000 to 3,000 of these feral chickens inhabit Key West and are perhaps more emblematic of the island than Jimmy Buffet, wild nightly parties, or the residents' notorious live-and-let-live attitude.

Possibly descended from fighting cocks brought to the island long ago, the chickens are protected by local law. They are not without controversy, however, and are once again at the centre of another kind of fight—between those who think they are a nuisance and those who feel they should be protected. Efforts to control the chicken population have met with varying success. An official chicken catcher, hired by the city back in 2004, was stymied in his efforts by chicken lovers who upset his traps. Other staunch defenders of the chickens include The Chicken Store on Duval Street, Key West's main drag, which has stepped in with its own Rooster Rescue Team, a volunteer group dedicated to aiding sick and troublesome birds and working towards greater chicken acceptance among island residents.

To many residents, the cats and chickens are an integral part of Key West's blend of Cuban, West Indian, Bahamian, and American cultures. Known for its history of pirates, who recovered treasure from sunken ships, and cigar makers, for its many 19th-century wooden homes, and as a haven for writers, artists, and those preferring less conventional lifestyles, Key West is unique among American cities. Tennessee Williams and John James Audubon, like Hemingway, fell under its spell, as did United States president Harry Truman, who chose Key West as the location of his Winter White House. A local nickname for natives of Key West is Conch, and the large sea snail from which the name derives is a local delicacy, often showing up as conch chowder or conch fritters. A tongue-in-cheek secession from the mainland has been proposed, declaring the independence of the Conch Republic.

There is an abundance of wildlife in and around Key West, of course. The island lies within the Florida Keys National Marine Sanctuary, created in 1990, and several national wildlife refuges are in the area. But even such exotic animals as alligators, sea turtles, and the endangered manatee, all of which can be found there, can't steal the limelight from the island's famous cats and chickens.

Atlanta, Georgia -- Animal control catches wild East Point chicken
From CBS Atlanta online, June 13, 2011, by Steve Kiggins

Fulton County animal control officers caught one wild chicken Wednesday.

Phillips said officers would monitor the area and return if they continue to get complaints.

Chicken advocate Alex Soto said he wants the chickens to stay in the neighborhood.

"I have a huge problem with it because they make the neighborhood unique and special. They should come and collect all the cats," Soto said.

People in the Jefferson Park neighborhood of East Point said as many as 8 chickens have been free-ranging on their streets – and they want to keep it that way.

Neighbors say the birds have lived in a vacant lot behind a row of homes on Bryan Avenue after they escaped from a chicken coup almost three years ago.

But now, someone in the area complained about the rooster's crowing, and now Fulton County Animal Control has gotten involved. People here don't want the county to trap the animals -- they want the birds to stay a part of their community.

"They have been lovingly referred to as the Bryan Avenue rogue chicken gang," said Sheila Merritt. "They definitely belong to the community and we feel a sense of ownership and responsibility for them."

Robert O'Neely got a notice from Fulton County Animal Control Monday afternoon. The notice said someone in the neighborhood thinks the birds make too much noise.

"I hate that they're bothering some people," said O'Neely. "All you've got to do is chase after them. They don't like people at all."

Chickens of Kauai, Hawaii

Wild chickens have inhabited the island of Kauai for over 1300 years. The first Polynesians to settle Hawaii brought chickens and small hogs in their canoes. The original chickens were similar in appearance to the Red Junglefowl but had been domesticated. As other breeds of chickens were introduced by Europeans, the original Polynesian chicken became a mixed breed, but most Kauai chickens retain some of the coloration of the Red Junglefowl.

The mongoose was introduced into the other Hawaiian islands to combat rats in their sugarcane fields. The mongoose has not been brought to Kauai.   If the mongoose were introduced into Kauai it would decimate the population of wild chickens because it eats chicken eggs on the ground. As it stands, the wild chicken has no natural enemies on Kauai. The wild chickens have the support of the vast majority of the island's residents to be preserved as a part of Hawaiian culture.

Of course, there is disagreement of what to do about the chickens. Some people find them to be very annoying.

Pesky Poultry Irritate Some Kauai Visitors and Residents
From Hawaii News Now, online, undated, by Diane Ako

LIHUE, KAUAI (KHNL) - It's a foul problem that's ruffling the feathers of some on the Garden Isle: roosters and chickens. And lots of them. What's a sleepless person to do? Chickens at church, at the cemetery, and tempting fate by dawdling around Burger King. Apparently, this chicken wants to have it her way. These feathered friends annoy enough people that the county council hears about it regularly. Councilman Mel Rapozo says, "We've heard it all. I've heard a request we pass legislation to ban chickens. Suggestions to offer a bounty for anyone who can bring in dead chickens and the county can pay a price. Working with the community college culinary arts students to provide them all the chickens."

Turning citizens into banty bounty hunters? Rapozo says the ideas won't take flight. "Sometimes I get offended when newcomers tell me we need to get rid of the chickens because I think the chickens have a place here in our culture."

Critics find that eggsasperating. "If one of the roosters had the bird flu it'd only be a matter of time before you had it because there are so many roosters on the island," speculates visitor Kyle Kirschbaum.

But for now, local lawmakers say to get used to it. "It's part of this culture and we just gotta learn to live with it. I am not planning to do anything to legislate chickens away."

Dr. Becky Rhoads of the Kauai Humane Society says, "I have no idea how many feral chickens are on Kauai. I would be surprised if anyone knows. For the past two years we have been offering humane live traps for folks to capture and remove nuisance chickens from their property. This is very similar to the feral cat humane trapping programs on most of the islands with humane societies. We offer this program to offer a humane alternative to control nuisances caused by chickens. We don't want people to cruelly control nuisance chickens by shooting, poisoning, etc. Folks pay a $25 deposit and get to use the trap for two weeks at a time. When the trap comes back, they get the deposit back. Most feral chickens brought to KHS are euthanized as they are feral game fowl, not adoptable as pets. Occasionally we receive commercial laying hens caught in traps which are adopted out to farm homes. I know of no successful way to keep a rooster quiet so no, we don't have any tips for keeping them quiet."

FITZGERALD, GEORGIA WILD CHICKEN FESTIVAL

The town of Fitzgerald, Georgia is known for its annual Wild Chicken Festival. The Festival is complete with a festival queen, a firefighters' chicken wing eating contest and an evening concert.

The festival honors the hundreds of Burmese chickens that call Fitzgerald home. They were imported in the 1960's by the Georgia Department of Natural Resources. It was thought that the Burmese chickens might become a wild game bird much like the pheasants of northern states. Instead, the Burmese chickens quickly faded from the rural areas and migrated to the urban setting of Fitzgerald where they are either loved or hated, much like other chickens in an urban setting.

CONTACTS

1. United Gamefowl Breeders Association

2. American Poultry Association

CHAPTER ELEVEN – DOMESTICATED TURKEYS, ROCK PIGEONS, GOATS, SHEEP, GEESE, DUCKS and RABBITS

All domesticated types of these animals are non-native to the United States, except turkeys; all were brought by European settlers; some have gone wild to varying degrees; ability to hybridize with native species; nuisance populations.

TURKEYS

Turkeys have an interesting history. They are native to North and South America. The native bird is called the Wild Turkey (*Meleagris gallopavo).* The domestic turkey is given the same scientific name. The first Spanish explorers found that the Wild Turkey had been domesticated in Central America and Mexico. More recent archeological evidence shows that the indigenous people of the Southwestern United States also kept turkeys. (1)

The Spanish took turkeys back to Europe where they became very popular. The English selectively bred turkeys to become more similar to modern-day domestic turkeys. The English returned the domestic turkeys to the United States, completing the round trip. The first English turkeys to arrive in the United States were brought to Jamestown in 1607.

In the Colonies, domestic turkeys were often allowed to run loose in yards or penned. They were not prone to escape and, when they did, they did not survive in the wild against predators like the wolf, coyote, foxes, bobcats and even wild dogs. Domestic turkeys had lost several of the abilities that allow wild turkeys to survive in the wild.

Domestic turkeys are nearly incapable of flight; they have shorter legs and heavier bodies, so they cannot run as well; their eyesight is weaker; and their normal white color works against them in nature. (2) While capable of reproducing with Wild Turkeys, the domestic turkey seldom does so in nature.

ROCK PIGEONS

The common pigeon found throughout urban areas of the United States is properly called a Rock Pigeon. It is a domesticated version of the wild Rock Pigeon that still exists in Europe, North Africa and South Asia. The wild version is called *Columba livia*; the domestic version is called *Columbia livia domestica.* The two types can inter-breed.

Rock Pigeons were domesticated over 10,000 years ago. Many fancy breeds have been developed but most Rock Pigeons remain similar in appearance and size to the wild type – gray with two distinct black bars on the wings. It is thought that the first Rock Pigeons in North America were brought to Port Royal, Nova Scotia, Canada in 1606. (3) Not long after, many European settlers brought Rock Pigeons to the United States, either to be raised for food or as a pet.

If you see a pigeon, it is probably a Rock Pigeon. There are seven other species of pigeons in the United States, but most of them are limited to the southern tier of states or South Florida. The mourning dove is the only other pigeon to be found throughout the United States. It is mostly gray, smaller than the Rock Pigeon and less common in urban areas. (4)

The domestic Rock Pigeon, like house cats, fill a niche where human structures, food sources and other activity occur. While the wild Rock Pigeon nests in cliffs in its native habitat, the domestic Rock Pigeon in the United

States cannot make it in the wild. They nest exclusively on buildings, bridges and other structures made by humans.

Rock Pigeons have been domesticated for several purposes. A large white variety called "King Pigeon" is often used as food. Pigeons raised for food are called "utility pigeons", as a group. Many restaurants in the United States serve squab, which is the name for a young pigeon. Pigeons have been used as messengers. They have a natural homing sense which can be intensified by selective breeding. Prior to modern communications, messenger Rock Pigeons were an important means of communication in active battlefield conditions. Pigeons are pets. Many fancy breeds of pigeons have been developed. Exhibitions and shows are held in much the same manner as conformation dog shows. Pigeons are also bred to compete in aerial acrobatics and flying competitions. Each of these types of domestic pigeons is capable of surviving in the niche created by humans.

The domestic Rock Pigeon is so well adapted to its niche that it is often a nuisance because of its numbers. Aside from the nuisance factor, Rock Pigeons have a low level risk of transmitting diseases to humans. This risk is not considered high enough to justify control measures. Still, control measures are often tried. Numerous control measures, sometimes humorous in the extreme, are tried to reduce the aggravation from domestic pigeons. After several years of activity, the control measures generally result in no reduction in the pigeon population and are abandoned.

One well-documented example is found in the efforts of the city of Basel, Switzerland to reduce its population of Rock Pigeons. From 1963 to 1985 the city tried to reduce its population of 20,000 Rock Pigeons by shooting and other lethal means. They killed 100,000 pigeons over that time span. In the end, the population of Rock Pigeons in Basel had swelled to nearly 30,000. The Rock Pigeons had simply replaced the ones that had been killed and apparently improved their reproductive potential in the absence of the pigeons that had been removed. (5)

GOATS AND SHEEP

Goats and sheep were brought along with other farm animals on Columbus' second voyage to the New World. Both of these species were important to the animal agriculture of the European settlers.

However, neither goats nor sheep went wild on the island of Dominica. And they never went wild on the mainland of Mexico or the United States. They could not establish wild populations due to the presence of stronger predators such as the mountain lion, bears, wolves, etc.

Because of the predator population in Early America, goats and sheep were more closely tended than other farm animals. Horses, cattle and hogs were tended in the Open Range system, which allowed many of them to escape. Goats and sheep stood no chance of survival if they escaped, so the settlers fenced them in, tied them up or ran them in naturally closed areas with close supervision.

Eventually, during the 1800's, much of the major predator population was eliminated from the United States. Mountain lions, wolves and bears were no longer a threat to goats and sheep. The last threats were the coyote and wild dogs. Coyotes and wild dogs kept goats and sheep from ever running wild in the United States.

Today coyotes and wild dogs remain as predators in every state, except Hawaii. Like wild hogs and pigeons, there are too many coyotes to eradicate. Farmers and ranchers who raise goats or sheep rely on fencing, poisons, guard animals such as llamas or dogs, shooting and habitat destruction to keep coyotes away from their herds.

Domestic goats and sheep have established wild populations in one state – Hawaii. There, they are a part of the unnatural Hawaiian "barnyard". They do not cause as much damage to the native habitat as wild cattle or hogs, but they are an unwanted presence. Efforts to remove goats and sheep from some areas of the Big Island have been successful. Goats, in particular, remain in areas used for big game hunting and are prized as a game animal by tourist hunters of Hawaii.

DOMESTIC GEESE, DUCKS AND RABBITS

As with all other farm animals, there were no domestic geese, ducks or rabbits in the United States before Columbus. Domestic geese, ducks and rabbits were imported from Europe. (6)

Geese, ducks and rabbits had been domesticated for centuries before Europeans came to the New World. Europeans had been selectively breeding geese, ducks and rabbits prior to bringing them to the United States. Fancy breeds and breeds designed for food were both brought by early settlers. In general, the improved European breeds were too domesticated to survive in the wild of the New World.

Geese

The European geese come from the Graylag goose. Its scientific name is *Anser anser*. Later introductions of domestic geese come from Chinese geese, *Anser cygnoides.* All of the current types of domestic geese come from the Graylag or the Chinese goose. Early settlers in North America tried to domesticate the Canada goose, but preferred the Graylag. (7)

Over time, domesticated Graylag geese have established breeding populations in the wild in the United States. There are reports that it has hybridized with Canada geese, on occasion. There are about a dozen other common domestic breeds of geese in the United States. None of them have breeding populations in the wild.

Ducks

The imported European ducks came from the common mallard, a species that is found in Europe and the United States. Its scientific name is *Anas platyrhyncos.* All of the fancy breeds of ducks can inter-breed with mallards. Hybrids are sometimes found in the wild, but do not achieve large populations. Domestic ducks are incapable of living in the wild because their ability to fly has been limited during the process of domestication. (8)

Muscovy ducks were imported from South America after they had already been domesticated there. Muscovy ducks are not related to mallards and do not inter-breed with wild mallards or domestic European ducks. The Muscovy scientific name is *Cairina moschata.* Muscovy ducks can revert to a wild condition and have become a nuisance in South Florida. Their range is limited and they are seldom seen in the wild.

Rabbits

All domestic rabbits in the United States are descended from the European wild rabbit, *Oryctolagus cuniculus.* They are unrelated to the American cottontail, *Sylvilagus floridanus.* They cannot inter-breed. If a domestic rabbit escapes in the United States, it will not form hybrids with the native rabbits. Small populations of the domestic breed can remain for a brief time in the wild. (9)

There are over 50 breeds of domestic rabbits and numerous more varieties within the breeds. None of them are able to survive in the wild of the United States due to competition from native rabbits.

CONTACTS

The only organized groups for turkeys, pigeons, goats, sheep, geese, ducks and rabbits are the breeders and producers organization. None specifically address wild populations. Of course, there are pigeon control companies in all major cities.

APPENDIX ONE

TALL TALES OF BONE MIZELL – FLORIDA CRACKER

COWBOY

From *Florida Cow Hunter*, by Jim Bob Tinsley (1990):

p. 73. According to Martha Kreider, scribe at the DeSoto County Courthouse, "He appeared in my record many times under the indictments for 'larceny of a domestic animal, to wit, a cow' but he told us once that the only time he was convicted was the only time he was not guilty."

p. 80. Bone once walked into a courtroom with his hat on and was promptly fined $20 by the judge. Bone calmly took two twenties out of his pocket, placed them on the table, and announced, "You better take forty, sir, 'cause I walked in here with my hat on, and I'm going to walk out the same way."

p. 84 and 85. Cy McClellan, another cowboy who worked with Bone, was known as a jester who would sometimes stretch the truth. Not wanting to be outdone, Bone remained on the alert for a challenge from him. One day, as the two were riding near Fort Ogden, Cy pointed across the vast ranges and pretended to identify a ship on the horizon. "Here comes the Matador," he said to Bone. "We been expecting her for some time now. Of course, she's pretty far out yet and I doubt as you can see her, mast and all." Bone studied the dry reaches to the west and replied, "Sure, I can see her, and there's a big horsefly on the mast." "By gosh, you're right," Cy answered. "I just saw him blink his eye."

The most famous of Bone Mizell's practical jokes spoke volumes about the attitude of the Cracker Cowboy.

The tale has been told in various ways. Here's an abbreviated version of the tale from pages 98 through 100 of *The Florida Cow Hunter*. This abbreviated version is probably as accurate as any of the other versions.

Bone was caring for a long-time friend, John Underhill, who had become gravely ill at an isolated cow camp. John Underhill was a poor Cracker landowner who had never left the state of Florida. When Underhill died, Bone and several friends buried him in a solitary grave out on the range.

Not long after that, a young man from a wealthy New Orleans family came to Florida to drop out of civilization. The young man had visited many countries and had tired of the New Orleans society and his many travels and thought he could escape to the frontier of Florida. The young man remained anonymous to his new-found Florida kin. Inexplicably, the young man teamed up with Bone Mizell for some of the range work. While with Bone, the young man became ill and died.

Bone and some friends buried him near John Underhill's grave. A few years passed before the youth's parents learned of his death and discovered that he was buried on the range in Florida. They immediately sent money to the local undertaker and asked that their son be exhumed and returned home for re-internment in the lavish family plot. The undertaker paid Bone to retrieve the body.

On the way out to the two unmarked graves, Bone did some thinking. He knew that the young man from New Orleans had been fed up with everything, most of all traveling. The young man had made it clear that he never wanted to see another railroad train and never wanted to go back home. Bone also knew that his friend John had always yearned to take a train ride and never had enough money to do it. Bone figured there was a free train ride ahead, a funeral so damned fine that Florida had never seen the likes of it – probably with four white horses pulling the hearse. Bone thought that John's reposing in a costly tomb would be a measure of justice. So he sent John to New Orleans, with nobody the wiser.

APPENDIX TWO

GREEN ISLAND, GEORGIA – AN EXAMPLE OF WILD CATTLE HUNTED FOR SPORT

Charles Hallock published an account of a wild cattle hunt on Green Island in Harper's Magazine in 1860. Hallock was widely recognized as an authority on field sports, fishing and conservation and the author of several hunting and fishing guides. He founded a leading outdoors magazine, *Forest and Stream,* and was an editor for several others. He helped establish the Bloomington Grove Park Association in Pike County, Pennsylvania, which was considered to be the first game preserve in the nation. He was involved in establishing conservation legislation in a number of states.

Here is a condensed version of Hallock's story of the wild cattle hunt.

I have selected only a short portion of his story to illustrate the exhilaration that the hunters felt during a wild cattle hunt and I have edited out or changed some of the language for clarity:

"All along the coast of Georgia the ocean sets into the land by numerous estuaries, creeks, and inlets, which, intersecting, form an extensive chain of fertile islands of great diversity in size and shape – some, whose large areas are monopolized by flourishing plantations; others densely wooded, with outlines sweeping gracefully into all conceivable curves, girt by the waters that float dreamily by. These are Edenal retreats, tenanted by lithe-limbed deer with large, loving eyes, and gaudy birds that flutter noisily amidst the interwoven foliage. Here the orange and palmetto grow in full luxuriance, the fragrant magnolia and huge live-oaks draped to their summits with long pendent

moss; and along the shadowy shores overhanging bushes, festooned with trailing plants, droop to the water's surface.

(On Green Island) there is a luxurious growth of young palmettos where the fields were once white with cotton blooms, and squads of Berkshire hogs, wild as the boars of Bohemia, roam freely and charge desperately into the cassena copses with a quick, sharp grunt when suddenly disturbed. Then, there are herds of Devon cattle of aristocratic blood, splendid animals, as wild as the lordly buffaloes of the Western prairies, but far more fierce and dangerous....These have grown wilder and wilder with each successive generation, until their natural fire has flamed into a restless passion, swelling the full veins that traverse their delicate skins, lighting their dark eyes with a malicious brightness and imparting a nervous quickness to their well-turned limbs. The haughty brutes are at all times ready to charge at whatever may excite their anger, or to dispute territorial possession with every living thing that crosses their path, and an open fight would defy the expertest matadors of Spain.

There is no gentleman's preserve in all Georgia so redundant in sport so exciting and deliciously dangerous, as is this hunting-ground of Green Island; and they are deemed fortunate who chance to be the recipients of an invitation from its proprietor, or members of his family, to participate in it. What thrill of pleasurable anticipation tingles every vein when the shrill horn calls "to horse!" How the mettled steeds themselves seem to catch the subtle inspiration, champing their impatience, and springing with nervous bound and fluttering pulse; and the whole crew of gathering dogs, of all degrees – bull-dog, hound, and mastiff – darting hither and thither in wild excitement, uttering eager whines and yelps!

(The dog handlers go down to the bayou with instructions to drive any wild cattle that they find toward the more open ground of the island.)

The horsemen clattered away to take their stand in waiting for the expected herd. No leather-clad hunter of the Far West was ever more properly equipped and armed than they; for each carried a pair of six-shooting revolvers and a heavy knife, and one or two had long barreled rifles; but these were intended more for certain contingencies than for active and general use. The pistols were the weapons to do the work, for the encounter was to be hand to hand and the stakes to be won were large.

The distant deep-mouthed bay of one of the dogs announced that the noble game is afoot. Then in one short instant more the exhilarating sounds are succeeded by an opening chorus from the whole pack of dogs. A momentary pause, broken only by the monotonous baying of a single dog, and another simultaneous roar of fitful yells comes nearer and clearer than before, and with increasing cadence. The sound is electrifying: the horses shiver with eagerness, and with ready alacrity bound away to advantageous points, the better to intercept the chase.

Now the chase bursts into full view through an opening in the trees – the bellowing cattle, some twenty in all, leading the vanguard, and plunging desperately forward in headlong terror…

The first onslaught has now commenced in real earnest, and the hunters, reckless of danger, dash in together amidst the surging tumult of horns and heels. The cattle, hitherto flying affrighted from an undefined danger, now charge savagely at their foes, since they have assumed a tangible shape; but the well-trained steeds skillfully elude the desperate brutes by a quick side motion, and, wheeling, follow on in swift pursuit. Crack after crack of pistol-shots is heard in quick succession, and the herd, now scattered, drive crashing through the young palmettos in all directions, each followed by a rabble of curs, biting and snapping at his heels and flanks, now pausing for an instant in his flight to charge upon his tormentors with stiffened neck, full front, and glaring eyes, tossing them like shuttlecocks from right to left, and then dashing away in the vain attempt to escape them.

(One hunter, known as the Colonel, loses his horse and is being chased, on foot, by the wildest bull in the herd)

The bull had so lessened the little distance between himself and the object of his pursuit that the unfortunate hunter now felt his hot breath full upon his bare neck behind; indeed, the brute was in the very act of lowering his huge head to give the requisite pitch to the quiver that was to toss his victim high in the air, when the Colonel, with remarkable presence of mind, took advantage of the proximity of a stout palmetto, and threw himself headlong behind the friendly refuge, while the foiled bull, with a howl of baffled rage, swept furiously by.

The Colonel was not hurt in the least, though he confessed himself to be badly scared. His steed fared worse, though he was found not dangerously hurt; and the big bull was discovered among those that had "bit the dust", when the noble quarry was counted at the close of the hunt.

APPENDIX THREE

GHOST OF THE RED CAMEL

From Faulk (1976), pp. 177-180

"The first notice of this animal came in the spring of 1883. At a lonely adobe house beside Eagle Creek in southeastern Arizona, two women and their children had been left alone when their men went to see about some sheep reportedly killed or stolen by Geronimo and his Apache warriors. During the morning one of the women went to fetch a bucket of water from a spring hidden nearby by willow trees. Dogs were prized by these people as lookouts for Indians, and one in the yard at this house suddenly began to bark so ferociously that the other woman ran to a window and looked to see what had stirred the animal. She heard the woman outside screaming, but she did not rush out to rescue for she saw something huge and red, seemingly ridden by a man – or devil. The woman inside barricaded the door and stayed inside praying earnestly until the men arrived."

"That night the men returned and, hearing the story, went outside with torches to search. They found the other woman dead near the spring and in the mud were cloven hoofprints twice as large as those of a horse. On the willows they found long, red hairs. A coroner was brought from Solomonville. At first he thought the family members must have killed the woman, refusing to believe the hysterical tale of the surviving wife; however, the severely trampled body and the hoofprints in the mud convinced him that the deceased had met 'death in some manner unknown'".

"A few days later and several miles to the northeast, two prospectors panning along Chase's Creek were awakened when their tent came crashing down on them. More frightening yet were the loud screams they heard along with thundering hoofs. Climbing from under the debris of their tent, they saw in the moonlight a very large animal moving rapidly away. They rushed to the nearby town of Ore where they told their story, and several miners returned to search the scene with them. In the mud along the creek they found huge footprints, and on the bushes leading away from the ruined tent they found long, red hair."

"Soon stories were circulating about a Red Ghost. Westerners loved a tall tale, and some raconteurs embellished the few known facts about this giant beast. One man claimed he had pursued the animal only to have it vanish before his eyes, while another told of seeing the animal kill and eat a grizzly bear. A month later Cyrus Hamblin, a rancher near the Salt River, went hunting stray cattle when suddenly across a ravine he saw a large red animal. In recounting the story Hamblin declared that the sight of the animal caused the hair to rise on the back of his neck, but he remained as the beast moved out into the open a quarter of a mile away. Suddenly he recognized the animal as a camel – and saw that tied on its back was something which resembled a man, but not one that was alive."

"Hamblin was widely known as a man of truth, but still the scoffers laughed. What he had seen was merely the camel's hump, they said. Then several weeks later and sixty miles away, five prospectors saw the same thing. Near the Verde River they came upon the camel with something on its back; they crept closer to get within shooting range, whereupon they opened fire. However, they apparently missed, for the animal was last seen running away rapidly.

During the camel's dash for life, the burden on its back fell off. Naturally the prospectors hurried to see what prize they had won. It turned out to be 'a human skull with a few shreds of flesh and hair still clinging to it'".

"This bit of physical evidence, when brought into Kingman, convinced even the skeptics that a huge red camel was running loose with the rest of the corpse tied to its back. Most concluded that some weary pilgrim, faint from thirst, had tied himself to the animal so it would take him to water, only he died before the camel felt the need to drink. Unable to free itself from this burden the dromedary retaliated by attacking all humans."

"A few days after the prospectors shot at this camel – he was no longer considered an apparition – a freighter and his helpers decided to halt for the night on the banks of the Verde River a few miles to the north. On the wagons were several kegs of whiskey; skeptics later could charge that their story was colored by their drinking some of what was on the wagons. Their version was that after they bedded down for the night, they suddenly were awakened by a loud scream, after which a giant beast at least thirty feet tall landed in their midst. This alone, they said, knocked over two of the wagons. The teamster, his helpers, and his mules fled into the night to remain hidden until daylight – and perhaps sobriety – revealed to them the source of their trouble. The next morning, when they found sufficient courage to return to camp, all they found were cloven hoofprints and red hair clinging to the side on one overturned wagon."

"Almost a year later a cowboy working east of Phoenix on the Anchor-JOT ranch came riding up to a branding corral which, at that time of the year, should have been empty. However, inside the corral was a strange animal eating the grass that had grown there. The cowboy had his lasso in hand, and as the huge animal came charging out he roped it. Only then did he realize that the beast was a camel, one headed straight for him and his horse. The horse reared and turned, as it normally would have done to escape a charging bull, but the camel did not keep charging by as a steer would have done; instead it hit horse and rider, knocking them to the ground, and then kept going. During all this the cowboy managed to notice that on the camel's back were the remains of a man."

"In the years that followed, stories about the Red Ghost grew in number, although the body tied to it had apparently come apart and fell off. Perhaps then the great camel became less vindictive towards humans and ceased its attacks, for no other stories surfaced about unprovoked rampages by the Red Ghost."

"Nine years later Mizzoo Hastings of Ore, Arizona, a rancher on the San Francisco River, awakened one morning to notice out his window that a huge red camel was eating his turnip garden. Hastings grabbed his rifle, steadied his aim on the window sill, and killed the Red Ghost. Everyone was convinced such was the case, for on the body was a patchwork of knotted rawhide strips, some of which had been on him so long that 'strands had cut their way into the flesh', according to the Mohave County Miner of February 25, 1893. An examination of the knots showed that they could not have been tied by the rider of so many years; the corpse had not once been a thirsty man trying to stay on the camel until he went to water. 'The only question is whether the man was tied on him for revenge,' asked the Miner, 'or merely as an ugly piece of humor by someone who had a camel and a corpse for which he had no use'."

BIBLIOGRAPHY

Akerman, Joe A., Jr. *Florida Cowman, A History of Florida Cattle Raising.* Kissimmee, Florida: Florida Cattlemen's Association, 1976.

Albright, J.L. *The Behavior of Cattle.* Madison, Wisconsin: CABI Publishing Series, 1997.

Allen, Lewis F. *American Cattle, Their History, Breeding and Management.* New York, New York: Taintor Brothers & Co., 1868.

Amaral, Anthony A. *Mustang: Life and Legends of Nevada's Wild Horses.* Reno, Nevada: University of Nevada Press, 1977.

Anderson, Virginia De John. *Creatures of Empire. How Domestic Animals Transformed Early America.* New York, New York: Oxford University Press, 2004.

Bancroft, H.H. *History of Alaska.* San Francisco: A.L. Bancroft and Co., 1886.

Belue, Ted Franklin. *The Long Hunt: Death of the Buffalo East of the Mississippi.* Mechanicsburg, Pennsylvania: Stackpole Books, 1996.

Beverly, Robert. *History and Present State of Virginia.* Charlottesville, Virginia: The University Press of Virginia, 1968.

Bowling, G.A. *The Introduction of Cattle into Colonial North America.* Morgantown, West Virginia: West Virginia University Agricultural Experiment Station Scientific Paper No. 277, 1941.

Bradshaw, John W.S. *The Behavior of the Domestic Cat.* Wallingford, UK, C.A.B. International, 1992.

Brookshier, Frank. *The Burro.* Norman, Oklahoma: University of Oklahoma Press, 1974.

Brennan, Joseph. *The Parker Ranch of Hawaii.* New York, New York: John Day Company, 1974.

Crosby, Alfred W. *Ecological Imperialism, Second Edition.* Cambridge, United Kingdom: Cambridge University Press, 2004.

Cruise, David and Griffiths, Alison. *Wild Horse Annie.* New York, New York: Scribner, 2010.

Dale, Edward Everett. *Cow Country.* Norman, Oklahoma: University of Oklahoma Press, 1942.

Davis, Karen. *More Than a Meal – The Turkey in History, Myth, Ritual and Reality.* New York, New York: Lantern Books, 2001.

De la Vega, Garcilaso. *The Florida of the Inca.* Translated and edited by John Grier Varner and Jeannette Johnson Varner. Austin, Texas: University of Texas Press, 1951.

De Steiguer, Joseph. *Wild Horses of the West: history and politics of America's mustangs.* Tucson, Arizona: University of Arizona Press, 2011.

Dobie, J. Frank. *The Longhorns.* Edison, New Jersey: Castle Books, 1941.

Dobie, J. Frank. *The Mustangs.* Lincoln, Nebraska: University of Nebraska Press, 2005, © Curtis Publishing Company, 1934.

Eklund, Beatrix. *Domestication effects on the social behavior of chicken (Gallus gallus).* IFM Biology, Linkoping University, unpublished manuscript. 2011.

Emmett, Chris. *Texas Camel Tales.* Austin, Texas: Steck-Vaughn Company, 1969.

Faulk, Odie B. *The U.S. Camel Corps, An Army Experiment.* New York, New York: Oxford University Press, 1976.

Fox, M.W. *Behavior of Wolves, Dogs and Related Canids.* London, U.K. Jonathan Cape, Ltd., 1971.

Gentry, Christine. *When Dogs Run Wild. The Sociology of Feral Dogs and Wildlife.* Jefferson, North Carolina: McFarland and Company, Inc., 1983.

Gohdes, Clarence, editor. *Hunting in the Old South. Original Narratives of the Hunters.* Baton Rouge, Louisiana: Louisiana State University Press, 1967.

Graves, H. B. *Behavior and Ecology of Wild and Feral Swine.* Journal of Animal Science. 1984, 58:482-492.

Gray, Lewis C. *History of Agriculture in Southern U.S. to 1860, v. 1.* Washington, D.C.: Carnegie Institute, 1933. Special Collection.

Harris, Joel Chandler. *The Complete Tales of Uncle Remus.* Boston, Massachusetts: Houghton Mifflin Company, 1955 (Original copyrights 1880-1948)

Haley, J. Evetts. *Charles Goodnight, Cowman and Plainsman.* Cambridge, Massachusetts: Houghton Mifflin Company, The Riverside Press, 1936.

Hallock, Charles. *Wild Cattle Hunting on Green Island.* Harper's New Monthly Magazine, XXI, 220-224. July, 1860.

Halloran, Art. *The Hawaiian Longhorn Story.* Hilo, Hawaii: Petroglyph Press, Ltd., 1972.

Heise, Laurie and Christman, Carolyn. *American Minor Breeds Notebook.* Pittsboro, North Carolina: The American Minor Breeds Conservancy, 1989.

Heptner, V.G and Sludskii, A.A. *Mammals of the Soviet Union, Volume II, Part 2.* Moscow, Russia: Vysshaya Shkola Publishers, 1972.

High Country News. May 26, 2008. *Rural West Going to the Dogs.* By Troy Anderson.

Horn, James. *A Kingdom Strange. The Brief and Tragic History of the Lost Colony of Roanoke.* New York, New York: Basic Books, 2010.

Housman, William. *Cattle. Breeds and Management.* London, UK: Vinton & Company, Ltd., 1902.

Jimenez, Juan Ramon. Translated by de Nicolas, Antonio T. *Platero and I.* Boulder, Colorado: Shambhala Publications, Inc., 1978.

Jordan, Terry G. *North American Cattle-Ranching Frontiers. Origins, Diffusion and Differentiation.* Albuquerque, New Mexico: University of New Mexico Press, 2000.

Keiper, Ronald R. *The Assateague Ponies.* Atglen, Pennsylvania: Schiffer Publishing, 1985.

Long, John Sherman. *McCord of Alaska: Statesman for the Last Frontier.* Cleveland, Ohio: Dillon/Liederbach, Inc., 1975.

Long, William G. *Asses vs. Jackasses.* Portland, Oregon: Criterion, Inc., 1969.

Loomis, Ilima. *Rough Riders: Hawaii's Paolo and Their Stories.* Waipahu, Hawaii: Island Heritage Publishing, 2006.

MacNeil, M.D., et.al. *Genetic relationships between feral cattle from Chirikof Island, Alaska and other breeds.* Animal Genetics, 38: 193-197. 2007.

Mayer, John J. and Brisbin, I. Lehr. *Wild Pigs in the United States.* Athens, Georgia: University of Georgia Press, 2008

MacDonald, David (ed.) *The Encyclopedia of Mammals.* New York, New York: Facts on File, Inc., 1984

McDonnell, Sue M. *Reproductive behavior of donkeys (Equus asinus).* Applied Animal Behavior Science 60, 1998.

McNitt, James, et.al. *Rabbit Production.* Danville, Illinois: Interstate Publishers, Inc. 2000.

Nowak, Ronald M. *Walker's Mammals of the World, Volume II.* Baltimore, Maryland: Johns Hopkins University Press, 1991.

Paskett, Parley J. *Wild Mustangs.* Logan, Utah: Utah State University Press, 1986.

Prioli, Carmine. *The Wild Horses of Shackleford Banks.* Winston-Salem, North Carolina: John F. Blair, 2007.

Porter, Valerie. *Domestic and Ornamental Fowl.* London, England: Pelham Books, 1989.

Rees, Lucy. *The Horse's Mind.* New York, New York: Arco Publishing, Inc., 1985.

Remington, Frederick. *Cracker Cowboy.* Harper's New Monthly Magazine, June, 1895.

Rouse, John E. *The Criollo. Spanish Cattle in the Americas.* Norman, Oklahoma: University of Oklahoma Press, 1977.

Ryden, Hope. *America's Last Wild Horses.* New York, New York: E.P. Dutton & Co., Inc., 1970.

Ryden, Hope. *Mustangs. A Return to the Wild.* Missoula, Montana: Mountain Press Publishing Co., 1984.

Schwartz, Marion. *A History of Dogs in the Early Americas.* New Haven, Connecticutt. Yale University Press. 1997.

Slater, Margaret R. *Community Approaches to Feral Cats.* Washington, D.C. Humane Society Press, 2002.

Smith, Andrew F. *The Turkey: An American Story.* Chicago, Illinois: University of Illinois Press, 2006.

Smith, Bruce D. *Subsistence Economies of Indigenous North American Societies.* Washington, D.C.: Smithsonian Institution Scholarly Press, Lanham, Maryland: Published in cooperation with Rowman and Littlefield Publishers, 2011.

Soule, Gardner. *The Long Trail: How Cowboys and Longhorns Opened the West.* New York, New York: McGraw-Hill Book Company, 1976.

Stone, Charles P and Anderson, Stephen J. *Introduced Animals in Hawaii's Natural Areas.* Proceedings of the Thirteenth Vertebrate Pest Conference. Davis, California: University of California, 1988.

Stong, Philip. *Horses and Americans.* New York, New York: Frederick A Stokes Company, 1939.

Time-Life Books. *The Cowboys.* Alexandria, Virginia: Time-Life Books, Inc., 1973.

Time-Life Books. *The Spanish West.* Alexandria, Virginia: Time-Life Books, Inc., 1976.

Time's Running Out for Wily Alaskan Cattle. Los Angeles Times, October 26, 2003.

Tinsley, Jim Bob. *Florida Cow Hunter. The Life and Times of Bone Mizell.* Orlando, Florida: University of Central Florida Press, 1990.

Tschiffely, Aime. *Tschiffely's Ride.* The Long Riders Guild Press, (orig.)1933.

Uncle Sam's Camel Herd. New York Times, January 12, 1896.

University of Arkansas Athletic Department. *Tusk: the Razorback Live Mascot.* Online Article, March 18, 2009.

Varner, John G. and Varner, Jeannette J. *Dogs of the Conquest.* Norman, Oklahoma. University of Oklahoma Press, 1983.

Walker, Stella. *Enamoured of An Ass.* London, U.K.: Angus and Robertson, 1977.

Wallace, John Hanks. *Horse of America.* New York, New York: Published by John Hanks Wallace, 1897.

Waring, George H. *Horse Behavior.* Norwich, New York: Noyes Publications/William Andrew Publishing, 2003.

Watson, Lyall. *Whole Hog.* Washington, D.C.: Smithsonian Books, 2004.

Wertenbaker, Thomas J. *Virginia Under the Stuarts, 1607-1688.* New York, New York: Russell and Russell, 1959.

Worcester, Don. *The Spanish Mustang.* El Paso, Texas: Texas Western Press, 1986.

Worcester, Don. *The Texas Longhorn. Relic of the Past, Asset for the Future.* College Station, Texas: Texas A&M University Press, 1987.

Wright, Hal and Lawrence, Rhett. *Feral Animals on Cumberland Island.* WildCumberland.org, 2010.

Wyman, Walker D. *The Wild Horse of the West.* Caldwell, Idaho: The Caxton Printers, Ltd., 1945.

Zarn, et. al. *Wild, Free-roaming Burros – Status of Present Knowledge.* Denver, Colorado. Bureau of Land Management, U.S. Forest Service Technical Note, Issued March, 1977.

Zarn, Mark et.al. *Wild, Free-roaming Horses – Status of Present Knowledge.* Denver, Colorado. Bureau of Land Management, U.S. Forest Service Technical Note, Issued March, 1977.

Zeder, M.A. *Domestication and early agriculture in the Mediterranean Basin: Origins, diffusion and impact.* Proceedings of the National Academy of Sciences 105(33): 11597-11604, 2008.

Zeuner, Frederick E. *A History of Domesticated Animals.* New York, New York. Harper and Row, 1963.

REFERENCES

PREFACE

1. Smith, Bruce D., pp. 543-551

CHAPTER ONE – HOLY COW! THEY'RE EVERYWHERE

1. Roberts, p. 458
2. Jordan, p. 70
3. Anderson, 2004
4. Jordan., p. 67
5. Rouse, 1997
6. Jordan, 2000
7. Jordan, p. 78
8. Jordan, 2000
9. Rouse, p. 202
10. Akerman, p. 1
11. De la Vega, 1951
12. De la Vega, p. 388
13. De la Vega, 1951
14. Heise and Christman
15. Rouse, p.18,19
16. Akerman, 1976; Jordan, 2000
17. Akerman, 1976; Jordan, 2000
18. Horn, 2010
19. Gray, p. 19
20. Anderson, 2004
21. Wertenbaker, p. 23
22. Anderson, p. 114

23. Anderson, p. 97
24. Anderson, 2004
25. Gray, p. 29
26. Gray, p. 234
27. Anderson., p. 207
28. Anderson, p. 232
29. Anderson, p. 79
30. Bowling, 1941
31. Gray, 1933
32. Gray, 1933
33. Dobie, 1941
34. Heise and Christman, 1989
35. Harris, 1955
36.. Jordan, p. 185
37. Time-Life Books, 1976
38. Time-Life Books, 1976
39. Time-Life (1976), p. 169
40. Halloran, 1972
41. Rouse, 1977
42. Allen, p. 38

CHAPTER TWO - THE TEXAS LONGHORN, THE PINNACLE OF BOVINE FAME

1. Rouse, Preface, p. x
2. Dobie, 1941
3. Dobie, 1941
4. Rouse, 1977
5. Dobie (1941), p. 49
6. Rouse, p. 192
7. Haley, 1936
8. Haley, 1936
9. Rouse, 1977
10. Dobie (1941), p. 33,34

11. Dobie (1941), p. 209

12. Texas Longhorn Breeders Association of America, internet reference

13. Dobie, 1941

14. Rouse, 1977

15. Townsend, p. 165 Dobie

16. Dobie (1941), p. 182

17. Dobie, p. 12

18. Rouse, 1977

19. Dobie (1941), p. 71, 72

20. Dobie (1941), p. 274, 275

21. Haley, 1936

22. Haley, 1936

23. Haley, 1936

24. Haley, p. 256

25. Dobie (1941), p. 117

26. Haley, p. 250

27. Allen, p. 175, 178

28. Allen, 1868

CHAPTER THREE – HORSES OF THE COLONIES

1. Anderson, 2004

2. Allen, 1868

3. De la Vega, 1951

4. Heise and Christman, 1989

5. Heise and Christman, 1989

6. Heise and Christman, 1989

7. Strong, 1939

8. Beverly, p. 312

9. Anderson, p. 135

10. Keiper, 1985

11. Gray, 1933

12.. Keiper, p. 14

13. Dobie, 1934; Keiper, 1985
14. Prioli, 2007
15. Prioli, p. 6
16. Prioli, 2007
17. Prioli, 2007
18. Wright and Rhett (2010)

CHAPTER FOUR – MUSTANGS, WILD HORSES OF THE WEST

1.   De Steiguer, p. 86
2.   De Steiguer, Dobie (1934), Ryden (1984), Wallace, Worcester, Wyman
3.   De Steiguer, 2011
4.   Dobie (1934), p. 108
5.   Dobie, 1934
6.   Amaral, p. 29
7.   Dobie, 1934
8.   Dobie, 1934
9.   Amaral, 1977
10.. Dobie (1934), Amaral, Paskett, Ryden (1984),Worcester, Wyman
11. Wyman, p. 259
12.   Dobie (1934), p. 111
13.   Paskett, pp. 3-7
14.   Amaral, pp 81-83
15. Tschiffely, p. xviii
16. Wallace
17. Haley, 1936
18. De Steiguer, 2011
19. Ryden, 1970
20. De Steiguer, p. 140
21. Zarn, 1977
22. Zarn, p. 9

CHAPTER FIVE – WILD HOGS, WHAT'S FOR DINNER?

1. Mayer and Brisbin, p. 3
2. De La Vega
3. Gray, 1933
4. Mayer and Brisbin, 2008
5. Anderson, p. 122
6. Mayer and Brisbin, p. 46
7. Mayer and Brisbin, p. 52
8. Graves, Mayer and Brisbin, Watson, MacDonald
9. MacDonald, p. 503
10. Watson, 2004
11. Mayer and Brisbin, 2008
12. University of Arkansas Athletic Department

CHAPTER SIX – INVASION OF THE CARNIVORES

1. Gentry, 1983
2. Schwartz, p. 30
3. Schwartz, 1997
4. Schwartz, 1997
5. Varner, p. 19
6. Varner, 1983
7. Varner, 1983
8. Schwartz, 1997
9. Anderson, p. 95
10. Anderson, p. 107
11. Fox, p. 194
12. Fox, 1971
13. Fox, 1971
14. Fox, 1971
15. Fox, p. 138
16. Fox, p. 156

17. Fox, p. 147
18. Gentry, 1983
19. High Country News, 2008
20. Gentry, p. 54
21. Gentry, 1983
22. Heptner, pp. 433-437
23. Heptner, 1972
24. Heptner, 1972
25. Heptner, 1972
26. Bradshaw, p. 9
27. Bradshaw, 1992
28. Slater, 2002

CHAPTER SEVEN – THE LOWLY BURRO, TOO COOL TO CHANGE

1. Brookshier, 1974
2. Brookshier, 1974
3. Brookshier, p. 221
4. Brookshier, p. 239
5. Long, 1969
6. Long, 1969
7. Brookshier, 1974
8. Brookshier, 1974
9. McConnell, Walker, Brookshier
10. McConnell
11. Jimenez, p. 12
12. Jimenez, p. 37
13. Zarn, p. 14

CHAPTER EIGHT – THE HAWAIIAN BARNYARD; COW ISLANDS OF ALASKA

1. Halloran, 1972
2. Brennan, 1974
3. Brennan, 1974
4. Brennan, pp. 21-31
5. Brennan, p.40
6. Loomis, 2006
7. Loomis, p. 14
8. Loomis, p. 15,16
9. Stone and Anderson, p. 137
10. Stone and Anderson, p. 137
11. Gentry, p. 84
12. Gentry, p. 85
13. Gentry, p. 136
14. Long, 1975
15. Associated Press (1985)
16. Los Angeles Times (2003)
17. Long, 1975
18. Bancroft, p. 352
19. Long, John
20. MacNeil, et.al., p. 196

CHAPTER NINE – CAMELS

1. Gray, 1933
2. Faulk, p. 35
3. Faulk, p. 48, ref Wayne to Davis, Constantinople, October 31, 1855, Camel File, OANRB.
4. Faulk, p. 55
5. Emmett
6. Faulk, p. 85
7. Faulk, p. 94

8. Faulk, p. 110
9. Emmett
10. Emmett
11. Faulk, 1976
12. Faulk, 1976
13. New York Times, 1896
14. MacDonald, 1984
15. Nowak, p. 1357

CHAPTER TEN - THE CHICKENS COME HOME TO ROOST

1. Porter, p. 17
2. Porter, p. 16
3. Porter, 1989
4. Eklund (2011)

CHAPTER ELEVEN - TURKEYS, PIGEONS, SHEEP, GOATS, GEESE, DUCKS AND RABBITS

1. Smith, Bruce D., 2011
2. Smith (2006), p. 40
3. Zeuner, 1963; Porter, 1989
4. Zeuner, 1963; Porter, 1989
5. Zeuner, 1963; Porter, 1989
6. Porter, 1989
7. Porter, p. 23
8. Porter, p. 21
9. McNitt, et.al., p. 5

www.ingramcontent.com/pod-product-compliance
Lightning Source LLC
Chambersburg PA
CBHW070858290526
45795CB00001B/166